LORD, I HURT!

THE GRACE OF FORGIVENESS AND

THE ROAD TO HEALING

Merry Christmas

Dr Castro

With ♡

Francesldy Smith

LORD, I HURT!

THE GRACE OF FORGIVENESS AND
THE ROAD TO HEALING

Anne Costa

Published by The Word Among Us Press
7115 Guilford Drive
Frederick, MD 21704

18 17 16 15 14   2 3 4 5 6
ISBN: 978-1-59325-200-7
eISBN: 978-1-59325-434-6

Cover design by Tim Green, Faceout Studio

Note: All the examples used in this book are based on real-life situations, and sometimes composites of several situations, in which the names and identifying details have been changed to protect confidentiality.

Made and printed in the United States of America

Library of Congress Cataloging-in-Publication Data

Costa, Anne.
  Lord, I hurt! : the grace of forgiveness and the road to healing / Anne Costa.
     p. cm.
  Includes bibliographical references (p.   ).
  ISBN 978-1-59325-200-7
  1. Absolution--Catholic Church. 2. Forgiveness—Religious aspects—Catholic Church. 3. Forgiveness of sin. 4. Healing—Religious aspects—Catholic Church. 5. Catholic Church—Doctrines. I. Title.
  BX2270.C67 2012
  234'.5--dc23
                                    2011046371

To my mother, Joanne,
with love
(without whom this book would never have been written).

Acknowledgments

Every book tells a story, and this one is no different. I am deeply grateful for the many people whom I interviewed and who unselfishly gave of their time and their hearts to share their experiences with me. Each one of you has contributed to this book and enriched my life in invaluable ways. Then there are the people who listened to me and supported me as my own story emerged and evolved through the writing of this book: Kathy Kreinheder, Adele Del Savio, Susan Storms, Paul Goggi, and my dear long-suffering husband, Michael, who continues to amaze me with his wisdom and his love.

TABLE OF CONTENTS

PREFACE

When the editor of The Word Among Us Press asked me what topic I might like to tackle for my next book, I pitched a few ideas, but none of them drew any interest. Then, knowing that I often speak to groups, she asked, "What are your audience members talking to you about?" And without hesitation I said, "They are hurting and struggling with the need to forgive." Needless to say, we had the topic for this book!

Where do you begin to write a book on forgiveness? Everyone, it seems, has some reason to be on the journey toward forgiveness because we can't live our human lives in this fallen world without hurting one another. Sometimes we act out intentionally, but oftentimes we hurt each other out of carelessness and our collective brokenness. Some of us have been carrying a heavy burden of hurt for a very long time, while others are just in the beginning stages of coping with a startling betrayal. Yet all of us, at one time or another, will be in need of healing from some form of emotional, physical, or spiritual pain. Many of us cry out: "*Why?* Why must I suffer in this way? Why must I forgive the unforgivable? And how can I ever forgive?"

If there is anything I have learned on my own personal journey of forgiveness and healing, it is that I may never know why. My persistence in asking that question over and over again at times of deep anguish and pain actually seemed to prolong the first steps toward healing. "Why" is not as helpful as "how": "How, Lord, *how* can I move from this place of pain and bitterness to freedom?" And then the prayer becomes this one: "Lord, please show me the way out of the darkness of my pain and the prison of my resentments."

This book is my humble attempt to help you answer the "how" question and to walk alongside you on the way toward a heart freedom that leads to forgiveness and peace in your spirit. Let me get one thing straight right away: I am not an expert—I still struggle with forgiveness too! In fact, I found the task of writing this book to be extremely challenging because I had to come face-to-face with some pretty uncomfortable feelings. I thought I had forgiven, only to find out that forgiveness is rarely a one time event, but more often an ongoing process.

Along with the challenge of writing this book has come the great blessing and gift of God's inspiration. Truly his Holy Spirit has guided my hand and my heart in a very powerful way as this book has unfolded. What I know for sure is that we are all on this journey together, and this is how the Lord intended it to be. We follow him with our crosses, but we are not meant to travel alone through this life. We are called to help one another as best we can.

There is no doubt that one of the most difficult crosses we carry is the one that won't let us forgive ourselves. You may be in the painful predicament of having passed an unmerciful and harsh judgment upon yourself long ago. Maybe you have grown accustomed to the heavy burden of pain and shame you carry. Perhaps you have refused the freedom that Jesus so dearly wants to give you because you have given up on yourself and on him. This book is for you too. Self-inflicted pain can be the worst kind of bondage, as it stands in the way of God's unending mercy.

Many people have contributed to this book by openly and honestly sharing their heartbreaks and struggles. I will forever be grateful and in awe of their examples of courage and vulnerability. I have learned so much from them—they have been my teachers, mentors, companions, and friends through the process of writing this book. I thank God for them all. These pages contain their stories. In many cases I have protected their identities for privacy's sake and changed some identifying details. In some cases I have combined the experiences of individuals to draw a composite of a common experience, but I have remained true to the heart of the original message and the spirit of each individual experience.

What I have discovered is that at the core of every story of forgiveness are Jesus and his cross. The whole of Christianity could never be believable without our dear and precious Lord, who was willing to enter completely into our brokenness and experience the same hurts, injustice, betrayal, and suffering that we encounter. And not only did he enter into it, but he took it all upon himself so that we, too, might have the hope and freedom to forgive.

Anne Costa

INTRODUCTION

*For I know well the plans I have in mind for you, . . . plans
for your welfare and not for woe, so as to give you a future
of hope. When you call me, and come and pray to me, I
will listen to you. When you look for me, you will find me.
Yes, when you seek me with all your heart, I will let you
find me, . . . and I will change your lot; I will gather you
together . . . and bring you back to the place
from which I have exiled you.*
(Jeremiah 29:11-14)

Of all the promises that God makes to us in his word,
this one has to be one of the greatest. In these verses
God spills forth a fountain of loving care and kindness. There is so much comfort here. He is planning for our
future. He cares about what happens to us and wants what
is best for us. And if things are going badly, he will change
the course of our lives. He will rescue us and bring us back
to him. God is with us; we are not alone.

There can be no better source of encouragement or hope than
knowing that we are not alone, especially when we are in pain
or experiencing suffering in mind, body, or spirit. Nothing feels
more like an exile than when we have been betrayed or deeply
hurt by someone or some circumstance in our life. If you are
reading this book, you probably know that already.

In fact, the experience of isolation and loneliness in our suffering may be so great that we cannot even begin to understand
or accept what God is saying here. That's okay. You don't have

to believe it just yet. Just keep it tucked away in your mind (and heart) as you read on. Consider that God, because he is God, has to keep his promises. He is Absolute Truth, and therefore, what he says is always right—he cannot tell a lie. So even if everything in your life or experience screams the opposite of what God says in this passage from the Book of Jeremiah, I urge you to just hang in there and keep on reading.

There are, no doubt, thousands of books that have been written on the topics of forgiveness and healing. Some of them are simple (too simple), some of them are scientific, and others could be considered theological masterpieces or psychological classics. This book will probably be none of the above! Neither is it a self-help manual; I can assure you that you will find no quick fixes here. It *is* meant to be used as a tool for self-reflection as you work toward healing, forgiveness, and freedom. Just know that I am writing this book with a deep desire and prayer that it will minister to you in a way that only the Holy Spirit can do, because he is the coauthor of this book. With his inspiration and my cooperation, we are writing this book together to help you on your journey of healing as you tackle what one writer called the "grunt work of forgiveness."

Lord, I Hurt! is divided into three parts. Part One explores forgiveness from a variety of perspectives. You will have an opportunity to reflect on the many facets of forgiveness and your own life circumstances. In Part Two, you will travel down the road to healing by examining the emotional conditions and experiences that can keep you bound to a lack of forgiveness. After each chapter you will find a section entitled "For Your Reflection" that includes a series of questions for you to consider or a short exercise intended to help you dialogue with God—in essence, to share your story with him as you so choose.

Before you begin these exercises, you may want to say a simple prayer such as the one I learned from Vinny Flynn, a Catholic author, presenter, and musician:

Come, Holy Spirit, come now, come as you wish.

You may also want to light a candle, bless yourself with holy water, or have a rosary or crucifix nearby. In doing so, you will be inviting the Holy Spirit into the process and creating a prayerful atmosphere and experience. Give yourself plenty of time for uninterrupted reflection, and be reassured that there are no right or wrong answers. You can even choose to forgo the "For Your Reflection" sections and not miss the main message of this book: that here is hope for healing and a promise of spiritual freedom for those who are willing to work through their hurts toward forgiveness.

In the first and second parts of the book, each of the chapters can stand alone as a complete meditation or "healing stop" on your road toward forgiveness and freedom. While you may choose to read the book from cover to cover, it is not necessary. It may even be more advantageous for you to prayerfully look at the chapter titles in the table of contents and let the Holy Spirit guide you to the chapter that resonates most with where you are right now. Throughout the book, you will hear the voices of people who have shared their experiences and stories of pain and reconciliation. Many of them are at a point at which telling their stories is an important part of their recovery; for some, it is the first time they have done so. We can't underestimate the healing power of sharing our stories with others, as it has the potential to help the listener (and in this case, the reader) just as much as the one who is sharing.

Part Three contains specific healing prayers and a list of resources for your personal, spiritual, and emotional healing. These are sources of information and support to which you may want to turn as you continue on in your journey toward spiritual freedom and peace.

THE GRACE OF FORGIVENESS

Forgiveness is a grace that comes from God and a gift that we give ourselves. Part One of this book will help you begin the journey of forgiveness that will lead you down the road to healing and spiritual freedom. One of the most important things that you can do right now as you begin to read is to remember to be gentle and patient with yourself, knowing that you are precious in God's eyes and loved more than you could ever know.

DEAR LORD, I HURT!

Behold, you desire true sincerity;
and secretly you teach me wisdom.
(Psalm 51:8)

Dear Lord, . . . I HURT!"
Other than "I do," these two short words have transformed my life more than any others.

I wrote them in my journal and finally said them out loud to myself after years of trying to run away from the overwhelming pain that I was in. I said those words just days after admitting that I was powerless over the substances I had used for the majority of my life to try and obliterate that pain. "Dear Lord, I hurt" became the prayer that launched my journey to find the truth and my very self, and I am still walking down that road toward peace and spiritual freedom today.

The journey has not been without its roadblocks and wrong turns, because facing the depths of my personal pain required that I give up the safety and security of my "false" self and all the things I did to pretend that everything was fine. To be stripped of my masks and "make-believe," with nothing but my past and present pain, was a very scary and lonely experience!

But that moment changed the course of my life, and it has transformed me and drawn me into a deeper, more loving relationship with God and others. This grace-filled healing toward wholeness from that moment forward has brought me the fulfillment of my deepest longings, one lesson in freedom at a time.

What I have learned will be shared in these pages, not just from my experience, but from that of others who, with courage and humility, have admitted their pain and set out on the long road to forgiveness and healing as well.

It seems obvious that before we can forgive, we have to acknowledge that we have been hurt, betrayed, or violated in some way. But a good deal of human suffering stems from the denial or the avoidance of acknowledging the deep pain that we are in. There is an old Chinese proverb that says, *"The beginning of wisdom is to call things by their right name."* Knowing that forgiveness requires more than a little wisdom, lots of time, and a healthy amount of emotional distance, our first step, then, has to be to name our pain. If we don't, we will prolong our agony. Unacknowledged pain can stunt our emotional growth, destroy our relationships, and even spill into the next generation. In short, denial of our pain becomes everybody else's problem as well. When our spirits have been hurt, our psyches damaged, or our hearts broken, we can't allow our pain to go underground. If it does, it will either erupt in a violent explosion or spill out slowly in our lives in a toxic manner at the most inappropriate times and circumstances.

In such cases, unforgiveness is the least of our problems. Instead, denial weaves a thread of destruction through our lives. We often hear of alcoholics or drug addicts who are trying to take the pain away, or of the abused child who grows up to repeat the cycle with her own children. These are the scenarios in which people have not faced their pain. They are the unhealed—the walking wounded—who have not integrated the painful and often unfair and unjust circumstances of their lives. They have yet to make peace with their pasts. Instead, the pain rages on beneath the surface of their lives. Dina, a retired schoolteacher, recounts an example from her own life:

My mother used to talk about her own father with the greatest admiration, even though he beat her mercilessly for the tiniest infraction throughout her childhood. Recounting the stories, she would laugh it off and make excuses for him.

The problem with this was that my mother couldn't see that she spent the rest of her life being mad at the world. She didn't see the connection to the fact that she heaped all of her rage on my brother and me. She drove my father out of the house with her drinking, and she went through life with a chip on her shoulder. Not even on her deathbed would she acknowledge that she was even angry at her father.

There is no doubt that the denial of pain can keep it buried alive and can inflict misery far beyond the original offense. Denial can also keep us from experiencing all that is good in and around us. Christian writer Stormie O'Martian puts it this way in her book *Finding Peace for Your Heart*: "As long as we rely on lies to insulate us from pain, we don't need to depend on God, and this will always keep us from experiencing all that he has for us."[1]

So why is it so hard to face our pain? After all, Jesus assures us in John 8:32 that "you will know the truth, and the truth will set you free." Why wouldn't we jump at that freedom? Maybe it's because, as President James A. Garfield once said, "The truth shall set you free, but it will make you miserable first." Many of us will go to great lengths to avoid that misery.

Etty Hillesum died in a Nazi death camp, but not before she had written down many of her thoughts, which were collected in a volume originally entitled *An Interrupted Life: The Diaries of Etty Hillesum*. Her words carry an eternal wisdom when she writes: "You must be able to bear your sorrow; even if it seems to crush you, you will be able to stand up again, for human beings are so strong, and your sorrow must become an integral part of yourself; you mustn't run away from it."[2]

However, to acknowledge our pain is to acknowledge our vulnerability, and this requires great courage. Especially if we experienced hurt or trauma early in our lives, our vulnerability can be experienced as life threatening. All of our defenses and denials were necessary back then to protect us. They were what helped us to survive things that were intolerable and harmful to our spirits. This type of "adaptation" to hurt and pain, whether it was emotional or physical, has the potential to shape us for the rest of our lives.

In fact, there is now a mountain of scientific evidence to support the idea that trauma, neglect, or abuse can affect our brains, and that even in adulthood, a single traumatic event can have negative physical consequences. As one scientist explained, "Our brains are sculpted by our earlier experiences. Maltreatment is a chisel that shapes a brain to contend with strife, but at the cost of deep, enduring wounds."[3] No matter how long we have been hurting or how pain has changed us, it will demand our attention at some point down the line. There is great wisdom in the words of French writer Marcel Proust, who said, "We are healed of a suffering only by expressing it to the full."[4]

If healing truly does come when we express the whole of our sorrow, then it gives us a good reason to find some way to do it. For some people, this comes naturally and flows from a trust that when they do express themselves, they will be heard and affirmed. The mechanisms they use to defend against expressing the depth of their pain are adaptive and flexible and help them to negotiate successfully through life. We all need these defense mechanisms from time to time to protect us from being consciously aware of a thought or feeling that we cannot tolerate. Yet if over time these defenses grow rigid and distort our present reality, they become psychological roadblocks that impede our ability to cope or come face-to-face with the truth of our experience—the truth that will ultimately set us free.

The Gospel of Matthew provides a very powerful example of Peter's use of a defense mechanism and how Jesus responded to it:

> From that time on, Jesus began to show his disciples that he must go to Jerusalem and suffer greatly from the elders, the chief priests, and the scribes, and be killed and on the third day be raised. Then Peter took him aside and began to rebuke him, "God forbid, Lord! No such thing shall ever happen to you." He turned and said to Peter, "Get behind me, Satan! You are an obstacle to me. You are thinking not as God does, but as human beings do." (Matthew 16:21-23)

From this passage we can see that Jesus became quite angry when Peter refused to face the truth. Peter not only wanted to avoid his own suffering at the thought of losing Jesus, but he tried to deny the reality of the situation that Jesus was in. This denial was something that Jesus even attributed to Satan—as something quite evil.

Here is another scenario that exemplifies how the major defense mechanisms are used:

Cassie was shy most of her life but managed to make a few friends along the way whom she really trusted, the closest of whom was Barb. She had known Barb since high school, and their friendship had endured through the tumultuous years of college and through their marriages and the raising of their children. As they faced the empty nest together, they provided one another with support through almost daily phone calls and lunches at least once a week. It seemed that their friendship couldn't possibly grow any closer. Then Cassie developed ovarian cancer. When Cassie found out, she was devastated, and one of the first people she told was Barb. But she was surprised, even startled, when Barb seemed to have little to no emotional reaction. In fact, it seemed as though Barb hadn't even heard her. Before long, it became clear that Barb was distancing herself. Even as Cassie entered chemotherapy, she never heard from Barb. Halfway through the grueling regime, she received a card, but it made no mention of the dramatic change in their relationship or what Cassie was going through. As a result of Barb's bizarre behavior, Cassie experienced a profound sense of betrayal and hurt and even stated that having cancer was less painful than losing her lifelong friend. Through tears and sobs, Cassie declared, "I will never be able to forgive her."

Remember, defense mechanisms are subconscious and often automatic reactions to intolerable situations or feelings. Our behavior is what people see on the outside. Here are examples of different defense mechanisms that Barb may have been using to deal with the pain and fear of Cassie's situation. These defense mechanisms are well documented;[5] here I have applied them specifically to Barb and the situation with Cassie.

Denial: A complete rejection of the thought or feeling.
"Cassie's not really that sick and she doesn't need me."

Suppression: A vague awareness of the thought or feeling, with an attempt to hide it.
"I'm going to give Cassie some space to deal with her problems."

Reaction Formation: Turning the feeling into its opposite.
"Cassie's going to be just fine. She's strong and can handle this."

Projection: Placing your thought or feeling onto someone else.
"Cassie has made it clear that she doesn't want me around right now."

Displacement: Redirecting your feelings to another target. *"I'm certain this lump is cancer."*

Rationalization: Coming up with various explanations to justify the situation (while denying it).
"Cassie's got her family and great doctors. They can do so much with cancer now. It's really no big deal, and she doesn't need me around, getting in the way."

Intellectualization: A type of rationalization, only more intellectualized.
"I read an article that said ovarian cancer is easily treated when it is detected early. The new drugs are powerful with very few side effects, and the article reported that the death rate has gone down considerably with early detection and treatment."

Undoing: Reversing or undoing your feeling by *doing* something that indicates the opposite feeling. It may be an "apology" for the feeling you find unacceptable within yourself.
"I'd better send Cassie a card."

Isolation of effect: Thinking instead of feeling the feeling. *"I think I'm a little nervous about the fact Cassie has cancer."*

Regression: Reverting to old, usually immature behavior to ventilate your feeling.
"Cassie's such a drama queen! I'm not going to feed into it."

Sublimation: Redirecting the feeling into a socially productive activity without addressing the original hurt.
"I'm going to volunteer at the American Cancer Society booth at the fair this year."

It's easy to see how using these defense mechanisms can lead to more pain for us and others. Most of us use one or two of these defense mechanisms regularly, and it is very helpful to know which ones we habitually employ to deal with unpleasant emotions and pain. With that level of insight and self-awareness, we can then prayerfully guard ourselves and seek better ways of coping. When we are able to discern our defensive style, then we can reflect and reframe, let go of habits and reactions that no longer work for us, and grow toward greater authenticity and freedom.

The flip side of denying our pain by pretending that we are not vulnerable or able to be hurt is to become overly sensitive and react to every difficult encounter or disappointment as a total disaster or rejection. We may be hurt to the core by the slightest "funny look" or provocation. We live life as a "walking wound"—a perpetual victim—or as someone who is offended by the slightest infraction. We wear our pain like a badge upon our chests, and we need—and maybe even expect— anyone and everyone to "pay" for the presumed and perpetual infliction of pain upon us. In this case, our vulnerability is magnified to an irrational degree within and around us.

Another way that we deal with unacknowledged pain is to try to control any potential for future pain. We do this either through perfectionism or people pleasing. Both of these activities are based on an illusion of control, that is, the erroneous belief that we can, by our actions, influence the outcomes, reactions, or actions of others.

There are many other strategies and patterns of defenses that you may recognize in yourself. Here's a list of some of them:

Blaming	Judging
Manipulation	Using humor or sarcasm
Bargaining	Shouting
Lying	Silence
Withdrawing	Smiling as a cover-up
Narcissism	Fantasizing
Arguing	Spiritualizing
Cockiness	Religiosity

This is not a complete list, but it does give us some food for thought. Which defenses do you employ most when you are confronted with very strong and unpleasant circumstances, such as fear, anger, violation, or pain? The most important thing to remember is that while our defenses may be necessary in the short run for psychic protection, they can lead us down a path of distortion and perhaps even greater pain if we rigidly and repeatedly use them to cover up the truth of our experience.

We started this chapter with a verse from Psalm 51:

Behold, you desire true sincerity;
and secretly you teach me wisdom. (verse 8)

Further along the psalm says,

My sacrifice, O God, is a contrite spirit;
a contrite, humbled heart, O God, you will not scorn.
(verse 19)

The truth is, we don't have to (nor can we really) hide our pain from God. The sacrifice that we are invited to make is to let go of our defenses and just "get real" with God. We can be assured that he does not despise our weakness, our brokenness, or our pain. *He will not put us to shame.* We can trust God with our deepest hurts and greatest fears. And when we do, he will teach us and give us the help and wisdom that we need to heal.

For Your Reflection

1. Prayerfully reflect upon one of your deepest hurts. Invite the Holy Spirit to give you the courage and strength to be honest with God and yourself about this painful situation. Tell your story of heartbreak to Jesus.

   Speaking your pain out loud or writing it down in a journal will help to break down your defenses, give voice to your secret pain, and respect the broken parts of you. This is an exercise between you and God. It will begin an important dialogue.

2. Review the many defense mechanisms mentioned in this chapter and identify, with the help of the Holy Spirit, which ones you use the most. As you bring these habits into your awareness, offer them as a sacrifice to God, and ask him to help you replace them with a more honest and direct means of dealing with your pain.

3. Put yourself in Peter's shoes in the passage highlighted in this chapter (Matthew 16:21-23). How would you respond if Jesus said those words to you?

CHAPTER TWO

WHAT IS FORGIVENESS?

"Forgive and you will be forgiven."
(Luke 6:37)

Every time someone breaks our heart, we have an open invitation before us in the shape of a cross. Jesus alone makes it possible for us to forgive. The cross is our reminder and our hope. It is a catalyst to set our faith in motion to enable us to forgive in a way that brings forth not only healing but a new wholeness that can lead to greater freedom and a deeper, more authentic love. This is the power, potential, and promise of the cross. But the cross also reminds us of the reality that we, too, must walk the way of Calvary as we struggle to make sense of our suffering and find a way to forgive.

Adding to our struggle is the fact that there is a great deal of confusion about what forgiveness truly is. We face many difficult questions: "What does it mean to forgive?" "How do I know when I have forgiven?" "Do I always have to forgive?" "What if the person keeps on hurting me?" All of these questions are valid and necessary, and for each one of us, the answers may be different. For all of us, forgiveness is a unique and individual journey. Every hurt, every wound, every betrayal begins a personal story with a potential final ending of forgiveness. How we write that story is up to us.

Too many of us, however, have been told that because we are Christians, forgiveness must be an automatic and instant response. Somehow this implies that forgiveness is easy, simple, and straightforward when, in fact, it is none of these. As people of faith, we certainly hope and pray that our heartaches and disappointments will ultimately help us to grow spiritually. Yet the only way that they can is if we allow ourselves to experience a glimpse of Christ's passion on our way to forgiveness. Instantaneous forgiveness rarely offers that opportunity. We can also acknowledge that as human beings, we all fail miserably at forgiveness when we try to go it alone. We need help, because true forgiveness is an act of grit and grace—our grit and God's grace! Forgiveness is a spiritual "work in progress" for most of us, even and especially when we are followers of Jesus Christ.

There are some important things to consider when asking the question "What is forgiveness?" As you read through this chapter, allow your heart to be expanded and your perceptions to be challenged. Be open to thinking about forgiveness in a different way. You may be holding on to some hidden misconceptions that are blocking your way toward healing and the resolution of your pain. Think of your present circumstances and the people that you need and want to forgive. Remember that the Holy Spirit is a source of guidance and truth for you. So as we begin, let's deal first with some misperceptions about forgiveness.

In order to forgive, I have to forget. For many, many years, I thought I had forgiven a person from my childhood who had hurt me very deeply. After hours and hours of spiritual direction and therapy, I felt reasonably at peace with what had transpired and certainly hopeful for my future in spite of the pain I had endured and the complications that it had brought with it into my adulthood. I felt that my success in life was a testament to the fact that I had moved on, forgiven, and forgotten—that is, until my daughter was born. The life-changing event of giving birth to an innocent, precious child stirred up an almost primal rage in me toward the person who had treated me badly when I was so small and vulnerable.

What I realized was that I had made some psychological progress and emotional adjustments. I had even gained maturity and insight into my situation. But I discovered that forgiving was the *last* thing that I had on my mind and heart! I had gone through the ritual of forgiveness without doing the real work. I had forgiven with my head but not my heart. I had placed my anger, resentment, horror, and brokenness neatly in a box marked "forgotten," tucked away in a dark corner of my heart, far from the light of Christ.

Now I know better. I know that forgiveness is a process, not a one time event, and that it is not helpful or even possible to simply forget. Forgetting the pain and the offense can be imprudent, especially when it might put us in harm's way, because our forgetting can lead to greater pain and bondage. Jesus wants more for us. South African Anglican bishop Desmond Tutu described it best when he said this: "In forgiving, people are not being asked to forget. On the contrary, it is important to remember so that we should not let such atrocities happen again. . . . It means taking what happened seriously, . . . drawing out the sting in the memory that threatens our entire existence."[6]

Forgetting is a vain attempt to bypass the "grit" part of the forgiveness journey. The truth is, there are layers upon layers of forgiveness. Like an onion, we must be willing to keep peeling back the defenses and false starts, letting Jesus our Savior get to the core of our hurt so that his hand of grace can lead us to complete freedom from our pain.

Forgiving means I'm "giving in." It often feels like forgiving means that we are giving other people permission to hurt us again or that we are condoning what has happened. At times, holding on to our anger feels self-righteous, and it gives us a sense of "evening the score."

When we have been hurt deeply, it seems outrageous to even think of forgiving because our trust has been shattered. We go into "protective mode" and do everything we can to stop any additional wounding. To forgive feels like adding insult to our already injured spirit. However, offering forgiveness is not an open invitation to get hurt again. It is an action that we take for ourselves. Forgiving allows us to move on and to let go of the hurt and pain. We can only do this when *we resolve to let go of our right to be offended* and relinquish our role as a victim. Far from weakening us, this choice empowers us to fully heal from our hurt.

I need to be free of bad feelings to forgive. When we choose to forgive, it doesn't mean that we will never again be angry or hurt by what happened. It doesn't even mean that we won't still be in great pain even as we take steps toward forgiveness. Forgiveness is a choice, not a feeling. So when we make that choice, it means that we will not allow those feelings to take up residence in our hearts, that we won't nurse our wounds and let them define us for the rest of our lives. It may even be that we make a decision to forgive long before we have the desire in our hearts to do so. Jesus can work with that. He can take our decision to forgive and infuse it with his grace. He will not be scared off by the raging storm of emotions that are stirred by the betrayal. As long as we are willing, he will guide us gently through those feelings when we are ready to get to the other side of the storm.

My offender must ask for forgiveness before I can give it. Or stated another way: "When so-and-so says he's sorry, then I will think about forgiving him." Our need or desire to have our pain and wounds acknowledged by the ones who have caused them has the potential to keep us stuck in our misery for a very long time, even a lifetime. You may have noticed that people rarely and sincerely ask for forgiveness. Many of the people who have hurt us are caught up in their own pain and may *never* come to terms with what they have done to hurt us. They may not even be aware of the damage they have caused, or worse yet, they may not care. They may acknowledge our pain but ask for forgiveness without a true feeling of contrition in order to ease their own guilt or to make their lives easier.

When we wait for an apology or even an acknowledgment before we forgive, we are giving all the power to the other person by making our sense of peace, joy, acceptance, and happiness contingent on his or her actions. Then we wonder why we can't get past our pain! It is because we are waiting for freedom from the wrong source. Our focus is in the wrong direction.

This is a very seductive way in which we bypass the need to forgive. We simply cannot afford to wait for someone else to restore our sense of well-being and peace. This is especially important for those of us who have to remain connected in some way to people who seem to be oblivious to our pain or who keep on hurting us, such as a family member or an employer. We have to find a way to forgive and function in these relationships without needing the offenders to understand, accept, or acknowledge our pain. We can only do this with the help of God's grace.

Forgiveness means I must reconcile with the person who hurt me. Forgiveness and reconciliation are not the same thing. We can forgive without remaining in relationship with our offender. We don't have to reengage with someone in order to forgive, and sometimes we shouldn't, especially if that person was abusive. Reconciliation requires two people to be "of one mind and heart," and that is not always possible. As Christians, we often fall into the trap of thinking that to love others as ourselves (Mathew 19:19), we need to be in relationship with them, even if the relationships are toxic or demeaning. You cannot resume a relationship with someone who hasn't taken responsibility for his or her part in the pain and division that caused the breach. That is not true reconciliation, because at the core of forgiveness are accountability and freedom. It is a responsible freedom that enables people to relate with integrity and to move in and out of relationships without strings or hard feelings.

For all Christians, true reconciliation is the goal whenever possible. Jesus stated this quite clearly in the Sermon on the Mount:

> "Therefore, if you bring your gift to the altar, and there recall that your brother has anything against you, leave

your gift there at the altar, go first and be reconciled with your brother, and then come and offer your gift." (Matthew 5:23-24)

This kind of reconciliation comes from God because it requires his restoring grace. We cannot accomplish this without his help. For many of us who have been deeply hurt or estranged for a long time, a vision of reconciliation may not even be possible. Yet God holds that vision in his heart, and he can make "all things new" (Revelation 21:5). What he needs from us is a willingness to be reconciled and an openness to a whole new relationship with the other person. His amazing grace will do the rest.

There is a "right" way to forgive. It would be so much easier if there were some simple steps or some magic formula that would bring about an easy and quick forgiveness. We all like simple solutions to complex human problems! But God doesn't usually work that way, especially when he is healing our hearts. The good news is that you can't "do it wrong." If someone tells you that your efforts to forgive aren't good enough or that you are less of a Christian because you find it hard to forgive, you can pretty much dismiss those words as misguided attempts to diminish the grace part of forgiveness.

However, there are some common characteristics of what forgiveness looks like and how it is experienced. Here are some hallmarks that indicate that you are on the road to forgiveness:

You no longer experience yourself as a victim. When we forgive, we trade our interior experience of victimization for the empowerment that comes from letting go of self-pity. Many of us are unaware that we are "victims" on the inside. While on the outside, we may appear happy-go-lucky, within our deeper core, we may feel perpetually wounded, mistreated, mistrustful, and misunderstood. Sometimes the root of rejection or betrayal runs deep within our hearts. Healing is ongoing in this area for many of us. Yet when we no longer feel like victims, we can let our guard down and begin to see and expect the good in others. We are more accepting of the failures and fallibility of others, and we let go of our defenses. Not being a victim means we are free from feeling powerless in the face of the injustices and sorrows of our lives.

You are free (most of the time) of the bitterness and desire for revenge. "Getting even has never healed a single person." Those are the words of Eva Kor, a Nazi Holocaust survivor who was featured in a 2006 documentary film entitled *Forgiving Dr. Mengele.* As one of the "Mengele twins," Eva survived the experimental torture inflicted by Nazi doctor Josef Mengele on approximately fifteen hundred sets of twins during the Holocaust. Eva also lost her parents and two other sisters and watched her twin sister, Miriam, endure lifelong complications as a result of the heinous treatment she received. What Eva has done with her life is nothing short of a miracle.

As a result of Eva's encounter with another Nazi doctor, Dr. Hans Munch, she is known worldwide as a forgiveness advocate. While searching for answers to treat the health afflictions of Miriam, Eva asked to meet Munch, and he agreed. It was during their conversation that Eva came face-to-face with the "enemy," and was able to witness, to her surprise, the impact of the Nazi atrocities on *him*. He was a broken and guilt-ridden man. It was in those moments that Eva realized that she had a much greater power at her disposal than her torturers could ever possess—she had the power to forgive. It was clear to her that by forgiving, she could be free of her resentment and bitterness far more easily than Dr. Munch could be free of his guilt. Since that meeting she has dedicated her life to promoting forgiveness and healing, not just for survivors of the Holocaust, but for all who have been hurt by life's injustices.

You can acknowledge some positive outcome or aspect of what has happened to you. God uses the weak to confound the wise (1 Corinthians 1:27); he uses our weaknesses to bring about his power (2 Corinthians 12:9); and he can take our deepest hurts and turn them into his greatest glory. This is the power of the resurrection and transforming grace of Jesus. In Romans 8:28, we are assured that "all things work for good for those who love God." As people of faith, we can cling to these promises from Scripture. There will be a point on the other side of our pain when we will have the distance and clarity to see the rose among the bramble bush of our experiences. In fact, many of the people who have shared their stories here have given their lives to helping others avoid or heal from the same kind of pain that they have endured. This is the blessing that flows when we accept God's healing of our deepest hurts.

You can pray for the person who has hurt you. This may mean that you have to ask *Jesus* to forgive that person or pray that the person goes to heaven. For many years I had to grit my teeth through these prayers. I had to admit that my feelings were not really in step with my words. Yet I knew that by praying, I was helping myself more than anyone else. Now, do I want those people who have hurt me to be in heaven? By God's grace, the answer is yes. Do I want to be sitting next to them at the banquet table? Not really, but God isn't finished with me yet!

You experience yourself as someone in need of forgiveness. This is an important step in our healing because it is the truth of who we are as human beings in the body of Christ. That shift of perspective, when we become more deeply aware of our own need to be forgiven, brings about a holy balance and humility. We begin to consider the injustice done to us in the context of the pain that we have caused others. Suddenly the evil that we experienced at the hand of another is tempered by our own awareness of the fact that we, too, have the propensity to cause harm or perpetrate evil. And we must beware of the temptation to think that we don't have that capacity. All of us need to be delivered from evil.

Remember, these are hallmarks, not requirements, so don't get down on yourself if you have not experienced any of these aspects of healing yet. One of the best definitions of forgiveness that I ever heard comes from a quote attributed to Corrie ten Boom, a Nazi Holocaust survivor, who said, "Forgiveness is to set a prisoner free, and to realize the prisoner was you." So think of these hallmarks as a part of your vision for the future as you seek freedom from your pain.

More than anything else, forgiveness is a decision, an act of the will that sets God's grace in motion. It is a commitment we make to be open to God's healing and transforming grace so that he can restore our broken hearts. Forgiveness is letting God rewrite our stories as we release the tight grip we have on our anger, resentment, and bitterness. We surrender our sense of entitlement to revenge, and we let God write the final chapter in our relationships. We allow reconciliation if it is possible. Forgiveness means letting love win out in our lives, just as it did on the cross on Calvary. *Forgiveness is letting Jesus into our hearts to set a captive free.*

For Your Reflection

1. Prayerfully consider what you believe about forgiveness, and then write five belief statements that begin with these two words: I believe_____. Be honest with yourself and the Holy Spirit about these statements, and take them to prayer. If some of these beliefs have become barriers to forgiveness, invite the Holy Spirit to put "a willing spirit" in you by praying Psalm 51:12-14.

You can have an enriching encounter with the living word of God in the psalms by reading, reciting, praying, and even singing them. Take some time to read as many of the psalms as you can because many of them speak to a heart that has been hurt by betrayal and the brokenness of humanity.

2. Psalm 69 was written by David, who is called "a man after [God's] own heart" (1 Samuel 13:14). In this psalm David pours out his heart in anguish over his enemies and pleads for God to take revenge on them. He also acknowledges his own weakness and inability to forgive. Consider writing your own psalm letting God know your true feelings about forgiveness.

3. Review the hallmarks of forgiveness listed in this chapter:

- *You no longer experience yourself as a victim.*
- *You are free (most of the time) of the bitterness and desire for revenge.*
- *You can acknowledge some positive outcome or aspect of what has happened to you.*
- *You can pray for the person who has hurt you.*
- *You experience yourself as someone in need of forgiveness.*

Do any of these statements describe you? Which one would you most like to embrace and experience? Are there any other hallmarks you can add to this list? Take some time to reflect upon or journal about any or all of these statements. Doing so will affirm your path toward forgiveness and encourage you along the way.

CHAPTER THREE

Why Should I Forgive?

*"Lord, if my brother sins against me,
how often must I forgive him?"*
(Matthew 18:21)

The short answer to "Why should I forgive?" is this one: "Because your Father in heaven says so!" But just as an "I said so" response doesn't satisfy our children, so it is not enough to convince most of us to jump right in and forgive those who have done us wrong. We need to dig deeper and explore the consequences of a lack of forgiveness in our lives.

It seems logical, even practical, to hold onto our stance of unforgiveness, especially in situations where we have been abused or betrayed. In these cases, our unwillingness to forgive may be a means of feeling safe or protected. We may believe that to maintain our dignity, we must never forgive. It is certainly true, as one Christian psychologist has said, that "forgiveness is not a natural act, but a supernatural one. We learn forgiveness through Christ, then attempt to exercise it in our relationships with others."[7]

God wouldn't command us to do something unless it was for our own benefit. His plans for us are always for our highest good (Jeremiah 29:11-14). He also wouldn't ask us to do anything that we couldn't do without his grace. St. Paul tells us to bear with one another, forgive whatever grievances we have against one another, and let Christ's peace reign in our hearts (Colossians 3:13, 15).

God knows that through obedience to his word, we will find true peace and happiness in life. As hard as it is to follow the path of forgiveness, the alternative is much worse.

During his public ministry, Jesus warned us against the consequences of hardness of heart and a lack of forgiveness: "Whoever is angry with his brother will be liable to judgment, and whoever says to his brother, 'Raqa,' will be answerable to the Sanhedrin, and whoever says, 'You fool,' will be liable to fiery Gehenna" (Matthew 5:22). Jesus also said, "If you forgive others their transgressions, your heavenly Father will forgive you. But if you do not forgive others, *neither will your Father forgive your transgressions*" (Matthew 6:14-15, emphasis added). Can you imagine what it would be like not to know the forgiveness of God? It means that we would live condemned lives. It is not God's choice for us; we are the ones who make that choice when we refuse to forgive.

So if we allow our anger to grow and fester, we open ourselves up to being judged in the same harsh manner in which we are judging our offenders. If we curse others or speak ill of them by allowing our tongues free rein to spew out negativity, then we must confess those sins in the Sacrament of Reconciliation. And if we persist in our anger so that it morphs into hatred and contempt, we run the risk of complete and permanent separation from God—we will never know peace again. Those are some pretty dire consequences for a lack of forgiveness in our lives.

But Jesus also warns us because he knows the terrible toll that a lack of forgiveness can take on our hearts. Unforgiving people often lead narrow, insulated lives. Over time they become petrified in their anger and resentment. They become stuck in a world of blame and often possess a chronically critical nature that reigns supreme. All of us know people like this, and we usually choose not to be around them. It seems that everyone with whom they come in contact must pay over and over again for the original unforgivable act. Unforgiving people are frozen in the pain of their pasts and simply cannot grow into the people that God calls them to be. As a result, they miss out on the abundant, rich life that he longs to give them.

There are also some practical reasons for us to forgive. There is mounting evidence that a lack of forgiveness is bad for our health. Recent research shows that those who can bring themselves to forgive enjoy lower blood pressure, a stronger immune system, less physical aches and pains, and a reduction in the anger, bitterness, resentment, depression, and other emotions that accompany the failure to forgive.[8] "Toxic" emotions such as chronic anger, hurt, guilt, and hostility create an excess of stress hormones such as cortisol, which can make us feel tense and overwhelmed and can impair cognitive ability. One study showed that anger-prone people are three times as likely to have heart attacks or bypass surgery as less angry people.[9]

One researcher from the University of Tennessee, Kathleen Lawler, was so struck by the health dangers of chronic anger and resentment that she looked to forgiveness as a way to stop the damage. In one of Lawler's studies, those who were "non-forgivers" were more likely to report illnesses and symptoms such as colds, infections, fatigue, and headaches and also took 25 percent more medications than those who had forgiven.[10]

These are all good reasons to forgive, but why does Jesus tell us to forgive "seventy times seven" times (Matthew 18:22, RSV) when to forgive even once seems so difficult? The answer is this: We should forgive because we are forgiven—and we are forgiven seventy times seven times by a merciful God who loves us. Seven is the number of infinity in Scripture. There is no end to God's mercy, just as there will be no end to our need to forgive others.

Forgiveness is the ultimate act of humility, meaning that through forgiveness, we discover our true selves. We come face-to-face not only with our own sinfulness but also with our own splendor as beloved children of God. This is a grace-filled turning point, as described by Claire, who experienced the power of forgiveness in her life:

> There was an anguished groan in my heart that wouldn't go away every time I thought of my husband cheating on me . . . and every thought was like a sword piercing my heart. I felt like I was going to be sick every time I even thought of forgiving him. And then one day, by some miracle of grace, I was suddenly aware of how much I needed forgiveness too. It was a turning point, a total relief.

Relief is a good reason to forgive. Whether we are aware of it or not, the weight and burden of *even one* instance of unforgiveness can affect every area of our lives. Martin Luther King, Jr., even went so far as to say, "Whoever is devoid of the power to forgive is devoid of the power to love."[11] The late Rev. Al Lauer, founder of Presentation Ministries and the religious community known as the Brothers and Fathers of Pentecost, dedicated his life to serving the body of Christ through the ministerial priesthood. On the Presentation Ministries Web site, he is quoted as saying this:

When I was first ordained a priest, I believed that over 50 percent of all problems were at least in part due to unforgiveness. After ten years in ministry, I revised my estimate and maintained that 75 to 80 percent of all health, marital, family, and financial problems came from unforgiveness. Now, after more than twenty years in ministry, I have concluded that over 90 percent of all problems are rooted in unforgiveness.[12]

Clearly, all of our relationships can potentially suffer from a lack of forgiveness on our part. We forgive seventy times seven times because forgiveness can't be selective, and believe it or not, the more we forgive, the easier it becomes.

Nevertheless, there *are* some instances when forgiveness is not appropriate. That is when forgiveness is premature, is counterfeit, or is used as a means to achieve some self-centered end. We must be careful not to use forgiveness to avoid a necessary confrontation or to control or manipulate others. Neither should we engage in forgiveness when it is part of a repetitive and destructive pattern, such as in the cycle of abuse. Forgiveness should never mean that you are giving someone permission to hurt or abuse you. Lewis Smedes, in his classic book *The Art of Forgiving: When You Need to Forgive and Don't Know How*, observed:

I worry about fast forgivers. They tend to forgive quickly in order to avoid their pain. Or they forgive fast in order to get an advantage over the people they forgive. And their instant forgiving only makes things worse. . . . People who have been wronged badly and wounded deeply should give themselves time and space before they forgive. . . . There is a right moment to forgive. We cannot predict it in advance; we can only get ourselves ready for it when it arrives. . . . Don't do it quickly, but don't wait too long.[13]

You may still be thinking of many reasons why you cannot or should not forgive in your particular circumstance. Yet consider this: By not forgiving, you are continually tied to your offender. There is an emotional bond that has not been broken yet. As clinical psychologists Henry Cloud and John Townsend note, "When you refuse to forgive someone, you still want something from that person, and even if it is revenge that you want, it keeps you tied to him forever."[14]

A lack of forgiveness helps us to keep a firm grip on our illusion of control. And it *is* an illusion. It helps us build a wall around our hearts to keep us from being hurt again. Yet that wall costs us dearly. When we don't forgive, we shut the door on God. We say no to the action of his grace to transform us and we turn our backs on the peace that he died to give us. Our hurts have the power to define us when we choose not to forgive. One unresolved conflict, one unforgiven act, one deeply inflicted wound left unattended has the potential to cripple our spirits and derail our lives. Why should you forgive? *Because you are the only one who suffers when you don't.*

The fact is, you can't forgive by fear or force. It must be freely given. Nobody, not even God, can compel you to forgive. You will have to take the first step on the journey. You alone must make the decision to forgive, and it is not something that can or should be rushed. Forgiveness is hard, and it takes time. The heart always knows when it is ready to forgive.

FOR YOUR REFLECTION

1. Pray to the Holy Spirit to guide you in this exercise. Take as long as you need to complete it.

    Get a large piece of paper or poster board and divide it in half. On the left side, make an inventory of your resentments; on the right side, list the corresponding impact that each resentment has had on your life. For example:

    Resentment:
    I am resentful that my sister made a scene and embarrassed me in front of the family last Christmas Eve.

    Impact:
    I haven't spoken to my sister since. Family gatherings are awkward, and I no longer look forward to them.

    Resentment:
    I hate my father for abusing me when I was child.

    Impact:
    I can't trust men and I can't have a lasting relationship no matter how hard I try.

2. Carefully and prayerfully review the impact and consequences of the resentments in your life. Choose one of them to take to the Lord in prayer, and invite him to heal the situation. Consider going through your list and repeating your request to the Lord one resentment at a time. Once you begin to see the negative and crippling impact of unresolved resentment in your life, the answer to "Why should I forgive?" becomes more evident.

3. Start a gratitude journal. In it keep track of everything that you are grateful for during the course of each day. While a lack of forgiveness constricts the heart, gratitude expands it and is an antidote for bitterness. It is doubly effective when you are grateful for the lessons you've learned through your interactions with the one you are struggling to forgive! Even if you are not yet convinced that you can or should forgive, gratitude can have a powerful effect on you and will go a long way in healing your hurts.

CHAPTER FOUR

FORGIVING GOD

"My God, my God, why have you forsaken me?"
(Matthew 27:46)

When Jesus uttered those words, he was in an agony that none of us can ever comprehend. He was taking on the sins of the world, and he was doing it alone. In his humanity he experienced the totality of what all of us should have suffered: the weight of our sin and complete separation from God. In comparison, our suffering will never be as great, but it will be enough to make us cry out just the same. We, in our own individual and collective agony, will most likely feel at some point the total despair and absence of God, just as Jesus did:

"My God, my God, where were you when I was being abused?"

"My God, my God, how could you take my child away from me?"

"My God, my God, how can you let this suffering go on?"

"My God, my God, why didn't you answer my prayer?"

When I finally came face-to-face with my own pain after years of abusing alcohol, this was the burning questions on my heart:

"God, *where were you?* Where were you when I was being hurt, and why did you allow me to be so alone, so scared, and so damaged for so long by circumstances that I could not control and that weren't my fault?"

Those questions didn't come all at once. In fact, it took several years for me to muster the courage to let those questions come up to the surface from the depth of my pain. As a Christian, I thought it was better to bury my anger toward God. I thought that it might even be sacrilegious to think that we have to forgive God for anything. After all, he is perfect and we are not. We are the ones that need forgiving. And while that's all true, I believe that God understands our humanity and our demands for an explanation. He knows that we will search desperately for the reason why we have to endure such pain and suffering; that we will shake our fists and blame him; that we will rail against him or quietly slip away from him as we deal with our confusion and hurt in the midst of our suffering.

I believe that God knows all this and still wants nothing more than for us to be reconciled to him. This "making peace" with God is an important and necessary step in our healing journey. All of our anger, fear, and grief bring us to this crossroad: How can we forgive God?

Each one of us will forgive God in our own way and in our own time. The most important thing is for us to receive the grace to *want* to let go of our hurt and anger so that we can forgive him. Our desire is enough when we don't know how and don't think we can let go. That desire will be the open door that God needs to soften our hearts and allow his living water to flow back into our doubting souls. When anger, fear, or grief brings us to a place of resentment toward God, or when we are at risk of losing or have lost our faith, then we are in great need of healing.

In a recent study, two out of three people in America said they have been angry with God at some point in their lives and have blamed God because they believed he was responsible for the bad things that happened to them.[15] So even though we may not admit it or talk about it much, most of us have or will struggle with anger and resentment toward God. Sometimes this will lead people into a "spiritual wilderness" experience in which they feel disconnected or unable to sense the presence or consolation of God in their lives. Other times people may engage in self-destructive behaviors because of unexpressed disappointments with God. Still others may simply curse God and turn completely away.

How we respond to God, in good times and in bad, has a lot to do with how we conceive of him in our heart of hearts. We all have deeply embedded assumptions about God that drive our behavior and affect our relationship with him. Some of these assumptions may even be subconscious, having been formed by such influences as popular media or childhood experiences that we haven't fully examined. In a book entitled *America's Four Gods*, two sociologists from Baylor University, Paul Froese and Christopher Bader, report on their survey findings of religious beliefs in America. They determined that while 95 percent of Americans believe in God, we view or conceive of God in one of four ways: authoritative, benevolent, critical, or distant. How we experience suffering or tragedy is influenced by how we view God.

Those who think of God as authoritative believe that he is engaged in their everyday lives and involved in judging their activities. They are most likely to view human suffering as a result of divine justice and may feel punished or cast out by God when things go wrong. Those who believe in God as benevolent also believe that God is very near but don't think that he is likely to punish them or judge their bad behavior. They will more likely feel comforted and will interpret God's "motives" as good. Those who believe in a critical God believe that he judges people's actions on earth but is removed from their everyday lives. They are less likely to blame God for what happens but will not seek or find comfort from him either. And finally, those who believe in a distant God do not hold him responsible for either bad or good things happening because they think of God as unreachable and uninterested.[16]

While we may hold certain assumptions about God and his character and involvement in our lives, it is important to remember that our thoughts may not be the reality of who God truly is. He reveals himself throughout Scripture, in the sacraments, and through our own life of prayer and interior contemplation. Be open to God showing himself who he is in your life. You will probably be surprised by what you learn about him.

Let me share with you a few things that I and others have learned when it comes to forgiving God.

Knowing why will not make the pain go away. When tragedy or injustice befalls us, our first reaction is to ask why. And we may get stuck there. In my situation, when my soul was in turmoil and my faith weak, my demands for an answer to the question "Why?" were my only form of prayer or conversation with God. For several years, it was pretty one-sided. I was so wrapped up in my questions that I couldn't hear his answers! We must be careful not to make our healing hinge on the need to have everything explained or understood. As I wrote in my first book, *Refresh Me Lord!*, "Freedom comes and life begins again when we release ourselves from the need to know the unknowable."[17]

God permits moral evil but does not cause it. The moral evil we suffer is not the result of anything that God has done or failed to do. God "permits it . . . because he respects the freedom of his creatures and, mysteriously, knows how to derive good from it" (*Catechism of the Catholic Church*, 311). The propensity of human beings to sin and abuse their free will results in suffering. We often blame God for the bad things that happen, as disgruntled children blame their parents when things don't go their way. To say this is not to trivialize moral evil but to take seriously the great gift of human freedom, God's goodness, and his abiding will to bring good from the horrendous evil human beings inflict upon themselves and one another. God always wants what is best for us.

Dave, who was abused by a friend of his parents when he was a small child, recalls his experience:

Deep down I knew that God would never want me to be abused, but I wanted, maybe even needed, to blame him anyway. I suppose in a way that it was safer for me to blame God than to blame my parents, who blindly entrusted me to the care of someone who turned out to be a monster. When I started to let go of my anger and even hatred toward God for letting it happen, I began to feel his love and care and concern, whereas before I had felt nothing but emptiness and distance. When I finally forgave God, he was then able to heal me slowly with his love.

God can see what we try to hide. Many times we try to hide our "bad" feelings and the resentments that keep us from making peace with God. Adele, whose son died in a surfing accident at the age of nineteen, explains it this way:

I think the biggest issue with forgiving God is the guilt that comes with being angry at God. Another issue, too, is our feeling of unworthiness or the fear that thinking God needs forgiveness is a form of hubris: "Who am I to think that a great being like God needs forgiveness from me?"

Adele suggests that visualizing Jesus in his gentleness might help because it could lead us to feel comfortable enough to express our anger and then our forgiveness. Maybe we might even be able to hear Jesus' apology, in keeping with the idea that God himself can't control everything and is sad when we are suffering.

God's love doesn't always come in pretty packages. Those were the words of a mother who had just lost her infant daughter after a valiant three-month struggle following a premature birth. Her daughter weighed less than a pound and a half at birth and had two major life-threatening defects as well as Down syndrome. The little girl's miraculous but short life brought the entire family, which included seven siblings, to their knees, literally and figuratively. Yet this was the encouraging message that this mother conveyed in a talk at a retreat for women just three weeks after her baby died: "When you are overcome by suffering, God *will* meet you there . . . *if you are willing*." One of the most powerful times that we encounter Christ is when we are going through the darkest, stormiest trials of our lives. Are you willing to seek Christ and accept his love, even when it is wrapped in the rags of suffering?

When we are mad at God or when we need to forgive him, I believe the person who can help us the most is the Holy Spirit. He is our Helper and Counselor. Call on him to act as an intermediary to negotiate the territory of reconciliation in your relationship with God. This reconciliation requires two things: honesty and openness. Blaming God for your suffering can never bring you the peace you want, but finding a way to forgive him will. The Holy Spirit will help you to find that way to forgiveness, and he will give you the grace to do it.

Remember that God sent his only Son to show us his desire to be one with us. We serve a God who came not as an all-powerful king but as a suffering servant. Jesus came here willingly to show his love for us by enduring unspeakable suffering. Far from being removed from us, God shows us through the cross that he is in complete union with us in our suffering.

That is, in fact, the answer that God gave me to my question, "Where were you?" God showed me, in a way that resonated in the very depth of my being, that he was there with me the whole time and that he was hurting just as much as I was during those dark and lonely years. God did not want me to be hurt, and through my healing journey, he has also opened up the eyes of my heart to see how very precious I am to him. But I am no more precious to him than you are.

Jesus would have suffered and died for you if you were the only person he ever created. He would have done the same for me. The Bible says that God doesn't have any favorites (Acts 10:34-35). That's because we are all his favorites. There is no limit to his love and no limit to his patience. So when you are ready to forgive him, he'll be waiting for you with open arms.

For Your Reflection

1. Complete this sentence from your heart:
   "My God, my God, _____."
   Spend some time writing or talking to God about your feelings surrounding your deepest hurt. Ask the Holy Spirit to illuminate any part of you that is resenting or blaming God for your past suffering or current pain. Pray for the grace to be honest with yourself and with God, remembering that he will meet you there . . . as long as you are willing.

   Next, write a prayer of personal forgiveness to God. It may be easier to address your prayer personally to one of the divine Persons: Father, Son, or Holy Spirit. Maybe you will want to address all three.

2. Contemplate the four views of God: authoritative, benevolent, critical, and distant. Which one best describes your thoughts?

Compare this with how the *Catholic Encyclopedia* describes God: infinitely perfect, eternal, true, intelligent, unchangeable, omnipresent, and a God of justice, wisdom, holiness, and truth.[18] How does this description of God affect your ability to forgive?

3. Take some time to read the Book of Job in the Old Testament. He is our biblical partner in suffering. Though he endured tremendous trial, he "turned away from evil" (Job 1:1, RSV). While reading his story, take note of how Job communicated with God in the midst of his darkness.

4. Spend ten minutes in silence contemplating a crucifix.

CHAPTER FIVE

MERCY: WHEN GOD FORGIVES

"O God, be merciful to me a sinner."
(Luke 18:13)

At the end of the last chapter, we explored the attributes and nature of God. Maybe you have wondered throughout your life what God our Father is really like. We know that he is probably not the old, wise-looking, white-bearded man that looks down on us from paintings on church ceilings. So how do we know God? We know that we are to love and trust God, but how can we sincerely do that unless we really know who God is and what he is like?

Moses had those same questions. Throughout the Book of Exodus, we can read the unfolding relationship between God and Moses. Moses repeatedly asks God to reveal himself so that he might know him. "Please let me see your glory!" Moses asks, and God answers by saying, "I will proclaim my name, 'LORD,' before you; I who show favor to whom I will, I who grant mercy to whom I will" (Exodus 33:18, 19). Later on, God calls himself "a God gracious and merciful, slow to anger and abounding in love and fidelity" (34:6).

These passages make it clear that mercy is God's very essence. In fact, Blessed John Paul II called mercy "the most stupendous attribute" of God.[19] That's a good thing for us, because the truth is that we all need God's mercy all of the time. Our healing will depend to a great extent on how willing we are to be open to receiving God's mercy for ourselves and others.

Here is Jim's story about God's mercy working in his life:

Growing up was hard because my father was an alcoholic and a compulsive gambler. I can't remember a day when there wasn't a fight between my parents or when there wasn't tension that you could cut with a knife. I realize now that my father was emotionally unstable, but as a kid, I was terrified to even be in the same house with him. I was ashamed and embarrassed by the fact that all of my friends had nice new things, and everything we owned was shabby and second-rate. So when I turned eighteen, I was happy to leave home to attend college halfway across the country.

I had worked all through high school to afford a car to get me there. I was planning on becoming an accountant with my sights set on the corporate world when I graduated. Just before the end of my freshman year, I got a frantic phone call from my mother, who told me that my father was "missing." He had been fired from his job (again) and had told her that he was never coming back. At that time my family had no food and was facing eviction. So I left college, driving all night to get home, and I never went back. My father never did come back.

I landed a job in a factory in my hometown and supported my mother and brothers and put both my brothers through college. In my twenties I met my wife, and we got married and started our own family. Soon after that my mother passed away. Over the years I had heard from one of my brothers that my father was living on the streets in a neighboring city, but there was never any contact with him. I probably wouldn't have known him even if I had seen him. Life went on, and I was doing well at the factory. I was head foreman and pretty comfortable with life.

When I was thirty-eight, there was a knock on my door late one night. I opened it to see an old man, a street person, standing before me. It took me several seconds to realize that he was my father. He explained that he was dying, that he had maybe three months to live. He wanted me to take him in.

Jim went on to explain what happened next:

I wanted to scream at him, but I didn't. I wanted to close the door, but I couldn't. A flood of what I can only call God's mercy overcame me, and I was filled with nothing but tenderness. I knew that it couldn't be coming from me because I had played this scenario in my head over the years, and it never ended up in a good way. But here was my father, and I only wanted to make his last days on earth pleasant. It was a miracle, and those final days truly did bring both of us to a better place.

There is no doubt that God's mercy helped to heal and transform Jim's relationship with his father and most likely brought healing to both of their hearts. In fact, the whole gift of God's mercy is that it can be life changing when it comes to reconciling us with others and those parts of ourselves that cause us shame and separation from God.

I learned a great deal about mercy when I spoke with Dave and Lucy, who endured the loss of their daughter through murder. Their pain has brought them to their knees many times, yet they have remained open to God's mercy. In talking about the person they believe killed their daughter, Lucy says, "I pray for him like I pray for my own children. I pray that he will repent, not to me, but to God." As hard and as almost unbelievable as this may seem, we must remember that "judgment is merciless to one who has not shown mercy" and that when we allow mercy to flow freely in our hearts, "mercy triumphs over judgment" (James 2:13).

Mercy is the medicine for broken hearts and shattered souls. God's love and healing transform us through the conduit of his mercy. But as Sr. Wendy Beckett says, "He cannot transform us if we insist on only offering to him our goodness, our successes, and our strengths."[20] In other words, we can try to bypass our need for mercy, but deep down, the truth is that our salvation and our very lives depend solely on the mercy of God.

There is no more beautiful or poignant portrayal of God's mercy in the Scriptures than the story of the penitent woman in Luke's Gospel (7:36-50). She enters the home of a Pharisee to recline at Jesus' feet, anointing him with her tears and an expensive perfume. She is unabashed in her great love and complete contrition, and as a result, her many sins are forgiven. I have spent many hours in prayer contemplating this woman. The one characteristic that she displays that challenges and moves me more than any other is the amount of trust she must have had in her heart. I believe it is what made her great love possible.

That is why I believe that the image of Divine Mercy, given to St. Faustina Kowalska, contains the words *"Jesus, I trust in you."* To be able to receive God's mercy and extend it to others, we must first have a measure of trust in our heart. We must trust in the power of God's mercy to redeem and restore us, and we must choose mercy over vengeance, trusting that God's justice is perfect and should prevail, no matter what has transpired or what we have endured. We must love God's way above our own and hand over our judgments, our condemnation, our rights to retribution, and all of our excuses, trading them for trust and leaning only upon his mercy.

St. Faustina was a student of mercy as Jesus instructed her through many years of personal revelations. His words are recorded in her diary, *Divine Mercy in My Soul*, which is filled with wisdom and guidance on the gift of God's mercy. In it she writes these words of Jesus: "I desire to grant unimaginable graces to those souls who trust in my mercy" (687)[21] and "The greater the sinner, the greater the right he has to my mercy" (723).[22] I once heard a priest say that Jesus is literally aching to show us his mercy in the confessional. Jesus would go to the ends of the earth to bring back any one of us who has strayed—after all, while we were still sinners, he died for us (Romans 5:8).

Jesus said, "Go and learn the meaning of the words, 'I desire mercy, not sacrifice'" (Matthew 9:13). In all of our lives, we will be given the opportunity to learn the hard lessons of mercy. We are all sinners, and we all will fall short of the glory of God (Romans 3:23). Mercy allows us to bear fruit in accordance with our repentance. It enables us to be restored and redeemed in spite of our missteps. Sin leaves a wound on our spirits that can only be lanced and healed by God's mercy. We can do nothing but seek his mercy for ourselves, and then we are called to offer it to those who have hurt us.

Have you noticed that this world seems to be sorely lacking in mercy these days? Even among Christians, it seems that we would much rather find fault, pass judgment, remain disgruntled, and nurse our resentments, not just on a personal scale, but within communities and even among nations. We are quick to blame and criticize and slow to forgive, the very opposite of who God is, what he does, and what he expects of us. Sadly, I've seen this played out in parish communities torn apart by closings, mergers, and the sexual abuse scandal. We need healing as individuals and as faith communities, from the highest ranks to the people in the pews. So where do we start? I suggest we start with mercy.

What do you think might happen if we each made the decision to—just once—extend mercy instead of condemnation when we are hurt or wronged? What if we offer our hearts as a living sacrifice, as Jim did for his father, and forgo our inclinations to withhold love and lay blame? What if we offer up our feelings of indignation and our cries of injustice and recognize that we, too, are sinners, in need of God's mercy? What do you think might happen?

I think the whole world would change, one blessed and merciful act at a time. And that is just what we all need. Mercy is an act of love, and it is also a condition of the heart. God's mercy flows into this world through us; *we* are the instruments of his mercy. Jesus has made it clear that we are to cooperate with his grace in bringing his mercy into this world. Here are his instructions to St. Faustina:

I demand from you deeds of mercy, which are to arise out of love for Me. You are to show mercy to your neighbors always and everywhere. You must not shrink from this or try to excuse or absolve yourself from it.

I am giving you three ways of exercising mercy toward your neighbor: the first—by deed, the second—by word, the third—by prayer. In these three degrees is contained the fullness of mercy, and it is an unquestionable proof of love for Me. By this means a soul glorifies and pays reverence to My mercy. (742)[23]

Many souls . . . are often worried because they do not have the material means with which to carry out an act of mercy. Yet spiritual mercy, which requires neither permissions nor storehouses, is much more meritorious and is within the grasp of every soul.

If a soul does not exercise mercy somehow or other, it will not obtain My mercy on the day of judgment. Oh, if only souls knew how to gather eternal treasure for themselves, they would not be judged, for they would forestall My judgment with their mercy. (1317)[24]

For Your Reflection
....

1. Read and reflect upon Psalms 130 and 131. Psalm 130 is known as a prayer for pardon and mercy, and Psalm 131 is about humble trust in God. Invite the Holy Spirit to speak to you, and journal about what he says through these passages.

2. Write a letter about trust to Jesus. Even if you are struggling with being able to trust him, pour out your heart and thoughts. He will listen without judgment. He will help you to trust.

3. This exercise will help you to bring mercy to the forefront of your mind and activities. Pick a period of time: a week, a month, or even longer, when you keep track and record the following: (1) times I needed mercy; (2) times I offered mercy. At the end of the time period, review the lists, and determine how the exercise has affected the way you think, feel, and act.

CHAPTER SIX

FORGIVING OURSELVES

*Then Jesus said, "Father, forgive them, they
know not what they do."
(Luke 23:34)*

Perhaps there is no greater miracle of mercy than when we are able to forgive ourselves. During most of the conversations I had with people in preparation for writing this book, the topic always seemed to come back around to how extremely difficult it is to forgive ourselves. We can stay in bondage for months, years, decades, and even a lifetime because of our refusal to accept God's forgiveness, mercy, and healing for our transgressions.

Dare I say that this inability to forgive ourselves could be a form of pride? It may be an indication that we are refusing to accept ourselves as imperfect beings in need of a savior. Humbly accepting our brokenness and propensity toward sin is step one in the spiritual life. In fact, it is the first beatitude: "Blessed are the poor in spirit, / for theirs is the kingdom of heaven" (Matthew 5:3). We enter into God's dwelling, we come into his presence, not by our strengths, but through our weaknesses. This means that if we refuse to forgive ourselves, then we are refusing God's entry into our hearts.

The Holy Spirit gave me an illustration of this truth one day as I was walking in a park by a lake near my house. I watched as a father and his toddler son were playing near the shore. The little boy was running around, shrieking with joy as toddlers do, when the father called out sternly, "Don't go near the water, son!" The little boy stopped in his tracks because that was exactly where he was heading—toward the shoreline.

Several minutes passed, and the father received a cell-phone call. As the father was momentarily distracted, the little boy took the opportunity to test his father's imposed limit and started running toward the lake. Spotting him, I sprinted toward the boy in an instinctive move to help out, but not before the father swiftly scooped up his son with a very emphatic "No!" The father had rescued the little one just in time. Yet the little boy would have none of it. He was twisting and thrashing against his father's embrace, crying and pushing his little body as hard as he could away from his father's. He did not want to be rescued! It occurred to me that sometimes neither do we.

We choose instead to wallow in the misery of our mistakes. We focus all of our energy and attention on our failures and unforgivable acts, all the while twisting and turning away from God's mercy. We trade the power and promise of his redeeming grace for self-pity and the burden of a guilt that he never intended us to bear. But there is hope! God loves us in our sinfulness, and we are called to this kind of love too. There are no unforgivable sins, only unconfessed ones, and there are no sins greater than God's mercy. God's forgiveness is an open invitation to us to forgive ourselves.

One priest has written that "not forgiving ourselves can be a self-deception."[25] Our own harsh self-judgments can lead us to give up on ourselves, as a lack of self-forgiveness indicates that we somehow believe that we are "too far gone" to be saved. If we believe this deception, then we have license to continue in our sinful ways. In essence, being "unforgivable" means that we can conveniently "avoid the challenge of growth and spiritual maturity."[26]

We are told that "there is no condemnation for those who are in Christ Jesus" (Romans 8:1). We are not to condemn ourselves any more than we are to condemn others. God's commandment, in fact, is to love our neighbor as ourselves, and this love of self includes taking up the challenge of self-forgiveness.

Christine had an abortion when she was seventeen years old. She wanted to keep her baby, but her parents did not even consider that option. Christine was a straight-A student with several college opportunities. Her future path was in motion, and her parents were determined that she continue along it. The boy involved was a casual acquaintance who quickly washed his hands of the situation in favor of his own impending future. Overwhelmed and defeated, Christine went through with the abortion.

Aside from the procedure, which was traumatic and painful, Christine endured nightmares every night for over a year that included the endless cry of an infant and her inability to find the baby in the midst of terrible storms and danger. "Something went cold in my heart that day [of the abortion]," Christine said, "and I felt nothing but fear and shame from that day forward."

When she went to college, Christine's life changed almost overnight. Away from the watchful eyes of her parents, she began drinking heavily and engaging in promiscuous sex. She went through a series of relationships with men who were very abusive, and Christine seemed to find herself in one dangerous situation after another.

When talking about this time in her life, Christine concluded that "because I had destroyed one life, I felt almost driven to destroy another—my own." Her reckless and self-abusive behaviors didn't stop after college as Christine grew increasingly depressed. Most people nowadays would recognize this pattern as post-abortion syndrome. Christine describes it as "trying to erase the shame." She goes on:

How do you forgive the unforgivable? Something in a mother dies when her child dies, but I kept on living, and it was a living hell. I knew the abortion was wrong, and I felt that I should have done something to stop it. I was old enough; I could have made that decision. It took half of my lifetime to forgive myself for aborting my baby. And I could never have done it if it weren't for my faith in Jesus and my encounter with his mercy. All those years of pain and suffering were not necessary, but I believe that God allowed them to show me that I could never forgive myself on my own power. I could only make a bigger mess of my life. It is because his love is for real and his mercy is greater than anything, even my attempts to destroy myself, that I can finally say I have forgiven myself.

There is a powerful passage in Scripture that outlines the reasons why we are called to forgive not just others but ourselves as well. It comes from St. Paul, who writes the following:

He indeed died for all, so that those who live might no longer live for themselves but for him who for their sake died and was raised. Consequently, from now on we regard no one according to the flesh; even if we once knew Christ according to the flesh, yet now we know him so no longer. So whoever is in Christ is a new creation: the old things have passed away; behold, new things have come. And all this is from God, who has reconciled us to himself through Christ and given us the ministry of reconciliation, namely, God was reconciling the world to himself in Christ, not counting their trespasses against them and entrusting to us the message of reconciliation. (2 Corinthians 5:15-19)

How is it that we can remain unforgiving toward ourselves in the face of this good news? It would mean that the passion of Christ was for naught. Our own judgment of ourselves is trumped by the saving grace of God.

Judas and Peter both betrayed Jesus, but it was Judas who denied God's mercy. If Peter had done the same, he may never have had the courage to face Jesus again. The Bible is filled with people who failed, and failed miserably. David committed adultery and arranged for the murder of his lover's husband (2 Samuel 11–12). Moses killed a man (Exodus 2:11-12). These two men were both used by God to perform mighty and wondrous deeds as part of the history of our salvation. What if they had been stuck in self-pity and had refused to receive the forgiveness of the Lord? God could not have used them, and that is why not forgiving ourselves can be considered the greater evil.

I have found one step of the Twelve Steps of Alcoholics Anonymous to be very important in the practice of forgiving oneself. After having admitted in step five "to God, to ourselves, and to another human being the exact nature of our wrongs," step six says that we are "entirely ready to have God remove all of these defects of character."[27] This statement cried out to me, urging me to put all of my energy into *letting go* of my critical, harsh self-condemnation instead of holding onto it. We have to be ready, *entirely ready*, to let God's mercy flow into our hearts for ourselves and for others.

Whatever we have done in the past is never as important as what God wants to do with our future. There is a wonderful saying that reminds us of this truth: "It is never too late to become who you could have been." God makes us new by the blood of Jesus Christ, and he can use every single moment of our lives to bring about his purposes and his good and perfect plan for each one of us. The only way that our mistakes become roadblocks is when we fail to receive God's mercy to transform them into something beautiful and meaningful, with the potential to even be helpful to others.

St. Paul tells us what Jesus said when he asked him to remove a persistent shortcoming that he referred to as a "thorn" in his side:

Three times I begged the Lord about this, that it might leave me, but he said to me, "My grace is sufficient for you, for power is made perfect in weakness." I will rather boast most gladly of my weaknesses, in order that the power of Christ may dwell with me. Therefore, I am content with weaknesses, insults, hardships, persecutions, and constraints, for the sake of Christ; for when I am weak, then I am strong. (2 Corinthians 12:8-10)

God uses our weaknesses to bring about his glory. St. Paul offers this assurance: "I am confident of this, that the one who began a good work in you will continue to complete it until the day of Christ Jesus" (Philippians 1:6).

There is nobody better equipped to help someone overcome the shame of adultery than someone who has walked down that road. The same holds true for abortion, robbery, murder, addiction, or any other struggle or sin that we face. In fact, our works of mercy toward others are only possible when we have first extended them toward ourselves. Just as our sins are never private, neither are our acts of redemption. Forgiving ourselves is imperative if we are to become instruments of healing in this world. God forgives you. Do you?

FOR YOUR REFLECTION

1. Prayerfully examine the roadblocks to God's mercy in your heart. What is standing in the way? What feelings, thoughts, or fears do you possess about forgiving yourself? After reflecting on these questions, complete these "if/then" statements:

I feel that if I forgive myself, then_____.

I think that if I forgive myself, then _____.

I'm afraid that if I forgive myself, then_____.

2. Read and reflect upon Romans 8:28-39. How does this passage speak of forgiving ourselves? What promises are contained in these words? How are we called to respond to the love of Jesus, even in our failures and trials?

3. Write a letter of forgiveness to yourself.

THE ROAD TO HEALING

God's transforming grace works through our willingness to forgive and opens the door to healing for us in mind, body, and spirit. There is much that we can do to participate in our own healing when we cooperate with God's grace and let the Holy Spirit guide us.

Part Two of this book will lead you further down the road to healing. It deals with four major areas that are often in need of God's healing touch: personal boundaries and the emotions of anger, fear, and grief. Let this help you to continue on your personal journey, as you explore the emotional conditions and experiences that may be acting as stumbling blocks to complete forgiveness and greater spiritual freedom in your life.

Chapter Seven

The Blessing of Boundaries

With all vigilance, guard your heart,
for in it are the sources of life.
(Proverbs 4:23)

Boundaries are the emotional fences that make genuine healing and forgiveness possible. Healthy boundaries are essential for us if we are to follow the commandment to "love your neighbor as yourself." We all need boundaries to survive, but we may not be aware of them and their importance in our lives. Many people experience pain and difficulty, especially in their relationships and throughout their lives, and don't know why. Oftentimes it is a problem with inadequate or damaged boundaries and the confusion that can result.

Boundaries affect our well-being, but how do we know if we have a problem in this area? To gain a better understanding, below is a list of some of the indicators of boundary problems, followed by a contrasting list of what healthy, intact boundaries look like. These characteristics are taken from psychological studies, as well as from my own counseling experience.

People who have boundary problems
- have trouble saying no.
- feel guilty when they express feelings or opinions that might conflict with those of others.

- are "over-the-top" people pleasers.
- feel that they have no power or control over what happens to them (they feel like a victim).
- avoid confrontation at all costs.
- spend a lot of time and emotional energy trying to figure out what other people want and need.
- are confused about their own needs, wants, desires, or feelings.
- can be "clingy" and dependent in relationships or have trouble developing close relationships.
- may be overly sensitive, touchy, or defensive with others.
- allow treatment by others that would be considered abusive by anybody else's standards.
- are often exhausted, anxious, and angry but would never admit it.

People without boundary problems
- are clear about what they can and cannot do, and make decisions based on what works for them.
- freely express their feelings and opinions in a way that is respectful to self and others.
- are concerned about others but are not motivated by a compulsion to please them.
- have a sense of personal power, self-worth, and confidence because they can rely on their own inner capacity to handle most situations, even difficult ones, with a solid sense of self.
- will confront situations as needed out of a sense of what is right and true or on principle, without unnecessary aggression, fear, or trepidation.

- are self-reflective and engaged with others but not overly concerned about what is going on with them. They "live and let live."
- know what they want, say what they mean, and mean what they say. They express themselves with clarity and authenticity.
- have relationships and connections with others that are balanced, mutually beneficial, and satisfying. They move freely within and among relationships without guilt, shame, or a heavy sense of obligation or pity.
- have a strong and positive self-image and are not deeply affected by the opinions of others.
- are intolerant of and do not accept behavior from others that is repeatedly hurtful, shaming, abusive, or controlling.
- are typically energized, content, creative, and hopeful, and share those qualitites with others

This is not a complete list, but it may be enough to spark some thoughts in your own mind of where you could use some help. If you see yourself agreeing with most of the descriptors in the first list, it may mean that you are in need of healing in the area of boundaries. Problems with boundaries have also been called "codependence" in the self-help and secular literature, with scores of books and Web sites devoted to overcoming the negative effects on our emotional health and relationships. There is a great deal of wisdom and help available on this topic, and some of those resources are included in the back of this book.

Many Christians struggle with erecting healthy boundaries because they think it goes *against* Christ's teaching to love others.

They think that in order to be good Christians, they should allow themselves to be taken advantage of, accept hurtful or abusive behavior, or totally disregard their own needs. However, having healthy boundaries is biblical, and if we want to reflect God to others, we will need to erect healthy boundaries that define us.

Healthy boundaries allow us to take responsibility for ourselves so that we can be in a position to offer our hearts, care, and concern to others in a balanced way. "Balance" is the key here, because when we overstep our bounds, taking responsibility for other people and situations that are not our business, then we are no longer being helpful or loving. When we cross that line, it becomes more about us and our needs and less about the other person.

Where can we turn for a model of healthy boundaries? We can turn to God himself and the Holy Trinity. "The concept of boundaries comes from the very nature of God. God defines himself as a distinct, separate being."[28] Within the Trinity, God has boundaries. The love between them does not dissolve the boundaries; in fact, it strengthens them, and there is no overlap. Each stands alone, yet joined.

With that model in mind, boundaries can still be a challenge in our lives. For instance, what does this mean for the mother whose child is a drug addict or the son who can never do enough to please his father? How does a husband cope with a cheating wife? How does a woman feel safe after being sexually abused as a child? All of these people will potentially have difficulties with boundaries. All of them will struggle with a sense of self and with understanding where they end and the other person begins. Early trauma and abuse, in particular, and coping with addictions, in general, are all red flags for problems with boundaries. Even if we have experienced none of these things, we may still need help and healing to ensure our boundaries are working for us.

First, we must be convinced that boundaries are a good thing to have. Let us turn to Jesus to show us the value of boundaries. During his public ministry, Jesus showed that he had clear and firm boundaries. He was constantly being followed, even hounded by others—friends and foes alike. When he said, "Foxes have dens and birds of the sky have nests, but the Son of Man has nowhere to rest his head" (Luke 9:58), Jesus wasn't whining. He was simply stating a fact for the people who were clamoring after him, wanting to be his disciples. Further on in the passage, Jesus explained that to be his follower, one must be decisive and focused.

> And to another he said, "Follow me." But he replied, "[Lord,] let me go first and bury my father." But he answered him, "Let the dead bury their dead. But you, go and proclaim the kingdom of God." And another said, "I will follow you, Lord, but first let me say farewell to my family at home." [To him] Jesus said, "No one who sets a hand to the plow and looks to what was left behind is fit for the kingdom of God." (Luke 9:59-62)

These Scripture passages show us how boundaries clarify our responsibilities and priorities. We cannot truly be who Christ calls us to be if we are constantly looking back or trying to do everything for everyone. People who have trouble with boundaries can't say no and can't put limits on the demands that others place on them for their time, attention, or energy.

Yet Jesus was a master at managing his energy. He became human, so therefore he had physical limits just like you and me. He routinely went off to a "deserted place" to pray and get away from the crowds (Mark 1:35; Luke 4:42), not allowing himself to become overwhelmed or depleted. Scripture shows us that even God Incarnate had to take a nap (Luke 8:23)! The truth is, Jesus knew how to take care of himself, and there is nothing "unchristian" about doing that. Boundaries increase our level of self-awareness and self-respect. Instead of being drained by life and our relationships, boundaries make it possible for us to nurture and respect ourselves and accept our own limits.

There is one passage in the Bible that gives us a clear example of the importance of boundaries when dealing with addictions. It is the story of the rich man from Matthew 19:16-22. (The account is also found in Luke 18:18-23.) In this episode, a man approaches Jesus to ask him how he might enter into heaven. Jesus reminds him about the commandments, to which the young man responds that he has kept all of them since he was a boy. Then Jesus tells him to go sell off all of his possessions and give the money to the poor. At these words, the young man becomes very sad and walks away.

Jesus knew that the man was addicted to his wealth, status, and material goods. He could not give up these idols. This is the way of all addiction; it is idolatry run amok in our lives. It happens when a substance, activity, or relationship becomes the primary god in our lives, taking over mind, body, and spirit.

What does Jesus do in response? He lets the young man

go on his way. He doesn't beg or plead with him; he doesn't attempt to manipulate the situation so that the boy won't leave. Jesus doesn't lose his sense of balance, peace, or inner well-being because this young man is choosing to remain addicted to mammon. I'm quite certain that he didn't drive himself crazy second-guessing himself or feel less like a savior because this young man chose not to take him up on his offer.

What Jesus did do was draw a firm "line in the sand" for the young man. He made his expectations clear and didn't waver in them, regardless of how the boy responded. Jesus did this out of a genuine love, for himself and the young man. Jesus couldn't compromise the truth to make the young man feel better, and he wouldn't take away the freedom the young man had in choosing to remain in bondage to his material goods (addiction). This is Jesus exercising a healthy boundary. This is what we might call "tough love" today. It is an important expression of healthy boundaries, and it is entirely Christian.

Many people believe that if they set boundaries in their relationships, they will create conflict, which they want to avoid at all costs. However, it is more likely that conflicts will arise as a result of *not* setting boundaries. That's because of the very nature of those who are "boundary breakers." These are the people that we encounter in our families, churches, and jobs who don't respect boundaries. They can wreak havoc in our lives, and their negative impact can only be avoided when we set boundaries. It's helpful to identify who these people are in our lives. (The terms that follow to describe such people are my own, but the categories are based on well-known and documented strategies used by "boundary busters.")

"Bullies" will never accept your no. They will pull out all of the stops to get you to do what they want you to do, and when they are frustrated, they can become abusive, controlling, and toxic. Bullies will often turn things around to make it look and feel like *you* are the person who is acting badly, who is in the wrong, or who is the one who should change. Bullies are aggressive manipulators who routinely violate boundaries.

"Clingies" are passive manipulators. They often rush into relationships, are extremely needy and self-centered, and will be inappropriately dependent upon others. Clingies can be "very nice people" who feign deep concern and compassion for others, but who truly cannot see beyond their own "bottomless pit" of need. Clingies will trick, cajole, or flatter you into a smothering and one-sided relationship that is in desperate need of healthy boundaries.

"Guilties" use guilt as a primary means to get their needs met and to get others to do what they want. Guilties can only be successful with people who have been conditioned to feel guilty for being a separate person or for having their own wants, needs, and feelings. Guilties often appear helpless but are usually inwardly angry people who manage to be "sweetly" disrespectful of the rights and boundaries of others through the guilt they try to impose.

"Pushies" are people who know how to push your buttons. They find out how they can "get under your skin" and use that method to get what they want out of the relationship.

Pushies are always looking for the upper hand in the relationship, and usually repetitively apply a pressure or strategy that violates or challenge the boundaries of others.

Here is an example: You and a professional colleague are involved in a work project together. You have to work collaboratively over a period of time to accomplish the task. However, you begin to notice that your co-worker seems to "selectively forget" assignments, conversations, and otherwise agreed-upon plans. Then she routinely remember things "differently," essentially rewriting her own history to keep you and the other team members off balance, questioning themselves, or just generally confounded and exasperated. Taking advantage of this strategy, she often looks in control at everyone else's expense. When confronted, she will cover up this behavior by saying that she is too busy to remember or will insist that she's right while others are wrong.

"Me-mies" are narcissistic people who are psychologically unable to comprehend the feelings or experiences of others. They also possess an extreme sense of self-importance; the boundaries of others mean nothing to them. Me-mies leave no room for the other in a relationship. You may feel completely drained, disappointed, dissatisfied, or used when you are in a relationship with a narcissist because such people are focused solely on their own needs, and they expect (and sometimes demand) that you do the same. In particular, if you are the child of a narcissist, you will most likely struggle with being able to erect healthy boundaries in your life.

When boundaries are violated or fail to be erected, a sickness of the soul prevails. I believe that a lack of boundaries is one of the primary sources of emotional and spiritual "disease" and even contributes to physical disorder and decline. Scripture says that the body is the temple of the Holy Spirit (1 Corinthians 3:16). Our bodies are our physical boundaries, and within these temples, the Holy Spirit is our helper to maintain the sacred spiritual boundaries that guard our hearts. If our physical or emotional boundaries have been violated or were never adequately formed, our spiritual ones will be damaged as well. For this reason I believe that the healing of our boundaries is an essential spiritual work.

God can help us heal, and he will work with us to repair and restore our boundaries. He does this in the context of our relationships—with him, with ourselves, and with others. We can't be healed of boundary issues in a vacuum. Scripture is filled with accounts that capture the essence of the healing power of relationships. One of the most beautiful examples comes from the story of the Samaritan woman at the well.

The encounter is the longest conversation recorded between Jesus and any other person in the gospels (John 4:4-42). Jesus begins by asking a woman for a drink. During the course of the conversation, the woman mentions that she has no husband, and Jesus reveals that he knows she has had five husbands and is currently living with a man. Yet the manner in which Jesus speaks to this woman does not bring her shame. Far from it! As a result of their encounter, she is relieved, renewed, and restored because he has seen her essence and reflected only goodness and acceptance back to her. The woman goes away, freely and whole-heartedly inviting others to meet Jesus the Messiah.

Just as with the Samaritan woman, Jesus can help us to "see ourselves rightly." We need to allow him to transform us through the renewal of our minds (Romans 12:2) so that we can see ourselves as he sees us. We need to pray for the blessing of boundaries in our lives. Boundaries are essential for our healing, and they are what make authentic forgiveness possible. Healthy boundaries give us the distance we need to reflect, process, and decide how to best respond to the pain and tragedies of our lives in a self-respecting manner.

Boundaries are not walls. Setting boundaries does not mean that you are building a fortress around your heart. Think of it more like a garden gate with the latch on the inside. You choose whom you allow to enter. If certain invited guests start trampling on the daisies and kicking the rosebushes, it is your job to show them the way out, to evict them from the garden. When you discover that they cannot appreciate the beauty and delicate nature of the carefully tended garden, only you can protect the property. You can accomplish this with a measure of firmness, even a gentle escort, as you let them know that their behavior is unacceptable.

The boundaries we set offer us the protection we need to enjoy the beauty that surrounds us; they will empower us in all our relationships so that we can be at ease and show our true self to others. With boundaries intact, we are safe, secure, and comfortable in our own skin, and life can flourish within us. This is the life God intended for us and the one we can have when we, as the proverb at the beginning of this chapter says, "with all vigilance, guard our hearts," keeping our healthy boundaries intact.

....

1. Failure to set boundaries is often the result of self-destructive messages that we tell ourselves. These inner dialogs are based on faulty conclusions that we've made in the depth of our hearts as a result of the way we have been treated in the past. This treatment, or some seminal crisis or trauma, brought us into conflict with our ability to express who we truly are at the core of our being. Some of these inner thoughts might be the following:

- *"If I say no, people won't like me or I'll be abandoned."*
- *"Expressing my feelings or showing others my true self will make others angry with me."*
- *"I can control the thoughts, feelings, and actions of others by behaving in a certain way."*
- *"My feelings don't matter."*
- *"I don't matter."*
- *"I'm not good enough."*
- *"I don't deserve to be happy."*
- *"I'm selfish for wanting to get my needs met."*
- *"I feel guilty when I take care of myself."*
- *"I must keep peace at all costs."*
- *"What other people think, feel, or want is more important than what I think, feel, or want."*
- *"I am powerless."*
- *"I am stupid."*
- *"I don't belong."*

Do any of these statements ring true for you? Does your behavior reflect some of these conclusions, especially within your close relationships? Reflect upon where these thoughts or assumptions came from.

2. Rewrite these statements as affirmations, instead of negative conclusions, and recite them every day for three weeks. For example, the first statement can be rewritten this way: "*It is important for me to say no so that others can be aware of and respect my limits.*" Then observe any changes in your attitudes or beliefs about yourself during that time period. Write these observations in a journal or share them with a trusted confidante or in prayer with Jesus or Mary.

3. This is an exercise of the mind that can also give you a visual image of boundaries working in your life:

Allow yourself to enter into a relaxed or prayerful state. Visualize a beautiful garden. Take as long as you like, and let your imagination create a detailed picture of this beautiful garden sanctuary in your mind. Next, imagine a gate or fence around the garden. Spend a good deal of time constructing this fence or gate. What does it look like? What is it made of? How tall is it? How does it feel to know that the garden is safe from intruders? How will you let guests into the garden? What does the doorway look like? Who can walk through, and who must stay outside?

Chapter Eight

Anger and Healing

There is an appointed time for everything, . . .
a time to embrace, and a time to be far from embraces. . . .
A time to rend, and a time to sew;
a time to be silent, and a time to speak.
A time to love, and a time to hate;
a time of war, and a time of peace.
(Ecclesiastes 3:1, 5, 7, 8)

Anger is the first step toward forgiveness. That piece of advice—one of the most helpful I ever received—gave me permission to feel my rage, and it gave my anger a purpose. Anger is such a strong and unpleasant emotion that it has the potential to derail us and lead us straight into sin. No one wants that, so many people are afraid of their anger and end up suppressing it in unhealthy ways. Still others are perpetually angry, even in bondage to its power. Wherever you fall on that spectrum, it is important to understand and learn how to deal with anger and give it its proper place in your life. In doing so, you will be less likely to fear it or justify it and more likely to confess it so that you can be free of its negative effects.

Five years ago, my closest friend committed suicide. As the first waves of shock and confusion subsided, I discovered that I was very angry. I was angry at the painful and tragic circumstances that led her to take her life, and I was angry at God for not delivering her from them. I was angry with myself for not seeing the warning signs soon enough (I am a social worker, after all). But what troubled me most was the anger that lasted the longest—the anger I felt *toward her*. I was mad that she gave up; I was enraged that she left me and all of the people who loved her and tried to help her. For a long time, I could not forgive her for depriving her children and her future grandchildren of the joy of her presence and of her wisdom, guidance, and love.

There were many people who didn't understand or want to hear about my anger toward my friend. One person told me that I was being selfish; another person was incredulous and declared me callous and uncaring. Anger is an uncomfortable emotion for many of us because it is not rational, is rarely "polite," and doesn't always make us look good in the eyes of others. Yet anger becomes just as much of a problem when it can't be expressed as when it is expressed inappropriately or all the time.

Buried anger turns to bitterness and despair. Denied anger can even make us sick, causing nervous system disorders, including chronic tiredness, apathy, and lack of concentration, as well as chronic physical problems such as back pain and digestive problems.[29] And trying to suppress and deny my anger toward my friend after her death only prolonged my inability to forgive her. It also got in the way of my ability to forgive myself and God for what had happened. I struggled because the anger I felt was "unpopular" and unacceptable to some.

But what would have been the consequences if, instead of suppressing my anger, I did the opposite and vented it inappropriately, letting it spill out into every interaction and conversation I had until I felt some sense of relief? Would that have been better? I hardly think so.

As Catholic Christians, we know that an angry person can have trouble being a charitable person; it is hard to be holy when you are holding a grudge. Nevertheless, anger is still one of the most misunderstood of all human emotions. Let's turn to the Scriptures to illuminate our understanding. What does God say about anger?

> Know this, my dear brothers: everyone should be quick to hear, slow to speak, slow to wrath, for the wrath of a man does not accomplish the righteousness of God. (James 1:19-20)

> Because of these the wrath of God is coming [upon the disobedient]. By these you too once conducted yourselves, when you lived in that way. But now you must put them all away: anger, fury, malice, slander, and obscene language out of your mouths. (Colossians 3:6-8)

> The ill-tempered stirs up strife, and the hot-headed cause many sins. (Proverbs 29:22)

> Wrath and anger, these also are abominations, yet a sinner holds on to them. (Sirach 27:30)

As I read these passages, an image forms in my mind of anger as fire. If we hang on to it, we will get burned, as the verse from Sirach says. Stirring up our anger through our thoughts and actions is like stirring the embers of a fire—it will create even more of the anger, not less, as the Book of Proverbs indicates.

Finally, anger should be contained (as a fire must) in order for it to be positive or "productive" in any way. However, it is difficult to "harness" fire. We need to be careful and respect the power and potential of anger in our lives.

It is important to understand that reflexive anger that flares up as an immediate emotional reaction to an event is *not* sinful because there is no consent of the will in this instance (see *Catechism of the Catholic Church*, 1767–1774). Anger becomes a problem when we hold onto it too long, when we willfully entertain it in our minds and hearts, or as St. Paul points out, when we "let the sun set" on our anger (Ephesians 4:26). When we do that, anger turns into a grudge, which is defined as "a strong, continued feeling of hostility or ill will against someone over a real or fancied grievance."[30] Another definition comes from one of my favorite quotes: "To hold a grudge is like being stung to death by one bee."[31]

I come from a long line of "grudge holders." It was just a fact of life that if someone "did you wrong," you didn't forget about it. I never realized the impact of that legacy until I got married. Inevitably one morning early in our marriage, my husband and I got into an argument. It must have been over something important because neither one of us was talking by the time we left for work. All through the day, I "stewed and chewed" and got more and more resentful of him and his "uncaring" attitude. My thoughts became increasingly irrational and negative so that by the time I returned home, I was ready to don boxing gloves. My husband, on the other hand, greeted me at the door with a warm hug and an apology.

You could have knocked me over with a feather! I was amazed and confused because I knew I had acted just as badly as he had in the heat of the moment. I could not believe that he wasn't angry. "It's done; it's over with" was his reply, and he *meant* it. He didn't drag it up at the dinner table or throw it back in my face the next day. In fact, it was as if the slate had been wiped clean—imagine that! I will be forever indebted to my husband for showing me a better way. Just realizing that there was a different way of behaving was half the battle. Grudges can become habitual and even automatic. Yet when that happens, we have a swarm of bees to contend with instead of just one. Here are some things to think about to help you let go of your grudges:

Leave the justice to God. Scripture tells us to "take no revenge and cherish no grudge" against others (Leviticus 19:18.) We can do this with much more ease knowing that God is in control and will ensure that perfect justice prevails in every situation at the end of time. We nurse our grudges with visions of revenge and "getting even." Every person will have to give an account before God for what they have done. Trust God at his word when he says, "Beloved, do not look for revenge but leave room for the wrath; for it is written, 'Vengeance is mine, I will repay, says the Lord'" (Romans 12:19).

Realize that grudges are not harmless . . . and you are the primary victim. You lose energy, a sense of well-being, and potentially your state of grace when you hold a grudge. Grudges are sinful and need to be confessed. Going to the Sacrament of Reconciliation will help you let go of grudges by giving you grace and the power of Christ to overcome this destructive way of thinking and behaving.

Avoid behavior that keeps the grudge alive. Ruminating, rehashing, or replaying the betrayal or action that caused you pain is not going to help you heal and move on. These are all mental activities that are better replaced by other, more affirming and constructive thoughts. Just as you have trained your mind to dwell on the cause of your grudge, you can train your mind to dwell on something positive, life-giving, and healing.

When you find yourself going back over the incident, quickly find a comforting mental focus. It could be a favorite photograph, a healing prayer, a Bible verse, or a poem—anything that will bring a measure of peace to your soul. Praise is a powerful weapon against sinful anger. As soon as you become aware of your negative thoughts, start praising God instead.

Put yourself into the equation. Have you ever been on the receiving end of a grudge? Perhaps you've been shut out of someone's life or made to feel as if you've committed an unforgivable sin. No matter how hard you try to make amends or restore the relationship, you have been met with a hardened heart. Not a very good feeling, is it? Since we are told to treat others as we would like to be treated, consider how you would feel on the other end of the grudge you are holding.

Know that freedom from grudges feels better than revenge. Revenge never feels as good as we think it will, and it's sinful, so it can never bring about anything good. Being able to get angry and get over it makes life less complicated and much more pleasant. In fact, it puts anger in its rightful place in our lives.

We are instructed not to let the sun go down on our anger because when it goes unresolved, it becomes a chronic state for us. And when anger becomes our primary emotion, it can cause a great deal of physical and spiritual damage. An analysis of findings from forty-four studies published in the *Journal of the American College of Cardiology* reported evidence of a definite link between emotions and heart disease. Anger and hostility are significantly associated with more heart problems in initially healthy people, as well as a worse outcome for patients already diagnosed with heart disease. The same analysis also showed that chronically angry or hostile adults with no history of heart trouble may be 19 percent more likely than their more placid peers to develop heart disease. Among patients already diagnosed with heart disease, those with angry or hostile temperaments were 24 percent more likely than other heart patients to have a poor prognosis.[32]

Anger often leads to other sins such as lying, cheating, calumny, or murder. Anger or wrath has the potential to separate us from God and his grace, and that is why it is included as one of the seven capital or deadly sins. When we give ourselves over to a spirit of anger, our souls are in jeopardy and we become subject to spiritual oppression and bondage. In this case, our anger has the capacity to develop into full-blown hatred.

Most people do not want to hate, but they feel helpless against its power. Still, harboring hatred in our hearts is like slowly poisoning ourselves to death. We have only to turn on the evening news to see its effects in our world today. It tears apart families and nations. Therefore, it is important for us, both physically and spiritually, to learn how to "do anger well." This may mean that we have to *unlearn* our angry responses to be free from the negative and sinful consequences that they can have on us.

The virtues that help most in dealing with anger are humility and self-control. Both of these are fruits of the Holy Spirit, along with love, peace, joy, kindness, goodness, generosity, gentleness, faithfulness, modesty, and chastity (Galatians 5:22-23). All of these fruits are available to us, through grace, as we discipline our wills to express them in our lives. This is pretty awesome when you think about it: The same God who created us and our emotions is ready and willing to assist us so that we can express them in a way that is dignified and helpful instead of harmful.

We are given the gift of God's love through the Holy Spirit, who pours it into our hearts (Romans 5:5). Just as you can't pour anything into a cup that is full, the Holy Spirit cannot pour God's love and mercy into our hearts if they are full of anger, hatred, or hostility. The grace of forgiveness may not be able to penetrate and we will not heal from our deepest wounds. Therefore, a proper and healthy expression of anger requires prayer and help (insight) from the Holy Spirit as well as *practice*.

Keep in mind that our emotions and thoughts are intimately connected and influence each other in powerful ways, either positively or negatively. They are like twins in a baby carriage. They can't go anywhere unless someone is in control of the carriage. That someone has to be you. So in order for us to go in the right direction, we must use our *will*, powered by the Holy Spirit, to push that carriage.

Let me explain it another way. How we feel is directly affected by what we think. And anger is most often the result of distorted thoughts that are fueled by a sense of interior inferiority or fear. In fact, anger is what is called a secondary emotion. This means that when we have an angry outburst, it is usually because of some other strong feeling that we felt first but have covered up with anger.

These primary or "first-felt" emotions are sadness or fear. They leave us more vulnerable and are actually more "risky" to express than anger. Over time we *learn* to respond in anger to cover up our pain or anxiety. We feel those strong feelings of fear or hurt mostly due to distorted or wrong thinking. We get locked into thinking and responding to the world in ways that are self-defeating and not true. This is the way that the evil one gets access to our emotions—through our minds. Some of the most common "faulty conclusions" are that "I'm a victim," "I'm incompetent," "I'm invisible," or "I'm rejected." The by-product of these negative thoughts and feelings is anger.

One way to manage anger is to stop, step back, and analyze the event or trigger that made us angry and then to raise our level of self-awareness enough to identify the feeling we felt first, before we got angry.

Here's one example. Martha's husband, Len, returned home from work and headed straight for the refrigerator, not even noticing that Martha had spent the afternoon picking up the house and even doing the lawn work that was Len's job. After getting a beer, Len sailed past Martha, mumbling something, and sat down in front of the computer. Martha felt her cheeks getting red and her jaw tightening. She came up behind Len and shouted, *"I guess you don't care that I've been busy all afternoon! Can't you even say hello?"*

While Martha was clearly expressing her anger, chances are that she was actually hurt by her husband's lack of interest and maybe even felt rejected in those moments before she reacted. You can probably guess where this conversation was headed. Len would turn around and say, *"What's your problem!"* or something worse to match Martha's anger, and that would be the beginning of a long night for both of them.

What could Martha have done instead? She might have taken a deep breath, even counted to ten. This would have given her time to "check on the twins" in the carriage or examine her thoughts and feelings. In other words, she would have been exercising her will to become more self-aware, which is something we must practice. She might have then determined, *"Ouch, this really hurts! I'm so disappointed that he didn't notice my efforts,"* or she might have even been able to think beyond her own borders and conclude that Len was having a bad day. If she was hurt, taking some time to "go to Jesus" in her heart with her hurt feelings would have helped her to approach Len quite differently. By then, she would have been in a better emotional place and would have had a little more insight and just enough distance from her original negative feelings to say, *"I wanted to do something special for you today so I mowed the lawn and cleaned the house—did you notice?"* To which Len might have responded, *"Oh, I'm sorry, I had a bad day and I needed to check something on the computer."* No matter how

Len responded, though, Martha could then proceed with the conversation with a sense of balance and positive perspective. Even if she was feeling sad or slightly annoyed, her will would be in the driver's seat, not her emotions, so she would be much better able to communicate with Len when he was ready or able to give her his full attention.

As a parent, I have come to realize that the times when I become most angry with my teenage daughter are the times when I am most afraid for her. For example, when she makes a bad choice, like turning her phone off when she is out with her friends so that I can't get in touch with her, I become enraged upon her return. She, in turn, matches my intensity, and I soon have a full-blown power struggle on my hands. I have not communicated a thing to her except that I am hysterically angry and out of control. But the times when I can raise my self-awareness (instead of my voice) to a level in which I recognize that I am actually afraid that she is going to get hurt or that something bad has happened to her, then I can stop myself from "flying off the handle" and approach her differently. I can stay calm and communicate with firmness and intent instead. I can say something like, "Honey, I am really afraid when I can't get in touch with you that something bad has happened, so you must keep your phone on the next time that you go out with your friends, . . . which, by the way, won't be for a while, because you're grounded!"

This is simply a statement of fact, and it doesn't invite her to join me in a shouting match. When I can honestly confront my own fear and express it directly, then anger can take a backseat to what is really going on in my heart. Anger is rarely instructive or helpful. It is almost always the result of distortion. As an emotion, anger is not sinful, but it has the potential to lead to sin and separation in our relationship with ourselves, others, and God. For all these reasons and more, we need to seek healing for our unresolved anger.

One man expressed it like this: "Anger is like carrying two heavy suitcases with no place to put them down." If we use this image, we can see that relief from our anger will not come from indiscriminately venting it by scattering the contents of the suitcases all over the place. Doing so only creates more of a mess. Neither will we find relief by pretending that we are not carrying the baggage at all. What we can do is "lighten the load" by putting the strategies from this chapter and the resources in the back of this book to work in our lives, through prayer and practice. Then it is easier for us to put down our anger and pick up compassion, hope, freedom, and understanding as we journey together toward our heavenly home.

FOR YOUR REFLECTION

1. What follows are three emotional continuums for sadness, anger, and fear. Each starts at "neutral" and progresses in intensity. Take some time to review these emotions and the different levels they portray. Do you have some others you could add?

Neutral→Disappointed→Sad→Sorrowful
→Heartbroken→Despondent.

Neutral→Frustrated→Irritated→Annoyed→Upset
→Angry→Livid→Furious→Enraged.

Neutral→Concerned→Worried→Stressed→Anxious
→Afraid→Overwrought→Terrified.

This is a self-awareness exercise to help you to identify the full range of your emotions. Write down each of the above emotions in an "I" statement in a journal. For example:

"I was disappointed when my girlfriend forgot to call me back."

"I am frustrated by the lack of follow-through by my co-worker."

"I am anxious about the doctor's report."

Take time to think and pray about when and how you feel each of these feelings throughout the day. In conversations with others, use these words to describe your feelings. Instead of automatically saying, "I'm mad!" take a moment to discern if there is something else you are feeling, and name that feeling.

2. Have there been times in your life when you expressed anger with positive results? How did that feel? Write a personal "anger pledge" by answering the question: How will I make anger work for me?

3. Write your own personal prayer asking God to help you express your anger without sin.

Chapter Nine

Freedom from Fear

I sought the Lord, and he answered me,
delivered me from all my fears.
(Psalm 34:5)

More than anything else, it is fear that will keep us from healing and wholeness. Fear can keep us from getting angry in a healthy way. Fear can keep us from facing the storm of our sadness. And fear will nearly always keep us from receiving and giving love in the way that God intends. Fear is a tool that the devil uses to keep us from being who God calls us to be and from experiencing the abundant life that Jesus promised us (John 10:10).

There is probably no greater bondage this side of heaven than the bondage to fear. It is a direct consequence of the Fall, going all the way back to the Garden of Eden, when Adam and Eve hid from God. Their fear was borne not of reverence, honor, and awe, which would have been proper and life-giving, but instead it flowed from a sense of shame, separation, and guilt. Because of original sin, we can still fall prey to this type of fear today. Fear blocks our spiritual freedom and the gift of peace that God wants to give us.

The kind of fear that I am referring to is not the "fight or flight" response that we all experience when we are in danger or have been violated in some way. This type of fear is both informative and protective. Fear can be useful in many ways, and it can even be a blessing. For example, when Scripture speaks of the "fear of the Lord" (which it does over fifty times), it is referring not to the destructive force and form of fear that "becomes a snare" (Proverbs 29:25), but of the humble stance of a creature as it relates to its Creator. In these cases, fear of the Lord is the beginning of wisdom (Psalm 111:10), prolongs life (Proverbs 10:27), is a way to avoid evil (16:6), and brings riches and honor (22:4). It is both a gift and a virtue, and is something to be extolled and sought after through prayer and obedience.

Fear becomes a problem when it is chronic and oppressive. We can be afraid of so many things. We can be paralyzed or provoked by fears of failure, rejection, or retaliation. We can be afraid of "being found out." We may fear success, intimacy, or death. The Scriptures make it clear that "perfect love drives out fear" (1John 4:18), so any of us who are striving to love as Jesus loves will need to come face-to-face with our fears.

At a particularly vulnerable time in my life, when I seemed to be at risk of being overtaken by what I now call a "tsunami of terror," I listed my fears. There were thirty-three of them, each more paralyzing and terrifying than the next. I knew that my fears had gotten out of control, yet I felt helpless to know what to do. So I wrote down my fears, put them in an envelope, and placed them under a statue of the Blessed Virgin Mary that sat on my nightstand. I gave my fears to my Blessed Mother, and what happened next is nothing short of miraculous.

Within four weeks' time, I found myself in a psychiatric hospital in the throes of a psychotic depression. To any observer, it may have seemed that fear had won out and completely overtaken me. I was not in touch with reality, and I was very, very sick. I was in this condition for over a month, encased and frozen in my fear. It took an army of prayer warriors, the right combination of medication, and a miracle of mercy to bring me back.

Amazingly, I wrote my first book during my recovery from that experience. As I healed, I became aware that for the first time in my entire life, *I no longer felt afraid*. Since God's ways are not our own, I will probably never know why God chose to deliver me from my fears during that time, but I can tell you that it truly *was* a deliverance. Since that time and to this day, I have not been afflicted or hampered by fear in any way, and my life has been completely transformed. As a result of that experience, I also know that when I go to the Blessed Mother for anything, she is efficient and prompt in her mediation. She knows what we need, and she doesn't hesitate to go to her Son to get it.

While you may not have ever experienced fear in the dramatic way that I did, fear can still have the potential to seriously affect your life and spiritual progress. Scripture describes fear as a spirit that doesn't come from God. As St. Paul reminds his friend and spiritual companion Timothy, "God did not give us a spirit of cowardice but rather of power and love and self-control" (2 Timothy 1:7). Because "one who fears is not yet perfect in love" (1 John 4:18), it is important for us to confront our fears, and the first step is to name them. Here are some common fears that many of us experience.

Fear of confrontation. Women especially seem to suffer from this fear. Many of us would rather "keep peace at all costs" than initiate a difficult conversation or set the record straight. However, as Christians we are charged to speak the truth in love, and sometimes that requires necessary confrontation. Timidity is not an option.

What I found most helpful in overcoming this fear was to study the manner in which Jesus dealt with the Pharisees, especially as it is recounted in the Gospel of Luke. Jesus was wholly intolerant of their behavior, and he went so far as to call them "blind fools" and "hypocrites" (Matthew 23:17, 23). We could all use a healthy dose of righteous anger over injustice and the effects of sin. An infusion of wisdom and courage from the Holy Spirit can help us overcome this fear, which is also connected with the one listed next.

Fear of what other people think. Many of us suffer from "approval addiction" and are controlled by the opinions of others. We all want people to think well of us, but sometimes we can fall prey to an inordinate need to be liked, noticed, and accepted by others. This can be an exhausting fear that feeds the development of a "false self" and leads us to even greater insecurity as we seek to please others instead of God. Jesus speaks about this issue when he says, referring to the Pharisees, that "they preferred human praise to the glory of God" (John 12:43).

It is this kind of fear that drove Peter to deny Jesus three times (Luke 22:55-61). Fear may have been the reason that the people of Jerusalem called for Jesus' crucifixion just days after proclaiming him king (Matthew 21:6-10; 27:20-26). Embracing and proclaiming the truth, no matter what the cost, is the mark of a mature Christian. This is a worthy goal to pursue, and we are more likely to reach it as we meditate and pray upon the love and total acceptance that Jesus has for us. His love, acceptance, and approval are all that we need. We are acceptable in his sight and secure in his love. "If God is for us, who can be against us?" (Romans 8:31).

Fear of failure or success. Clearly the roots of this fear are perfectionism and pride, and its cure is humility. When we are afraid to fail or succeed, it is because we are placing all the emphasis on our own efforts, strength, and abilities instead of on God's power and perfect will. The Bible reminds us that "every perfect gift is from above" (James 1:17) and that "it is God who is at work in you, enabling you both to will and to work for his good pleasure" (Philippians 2:13, NRSV).

The best way to combat this fear is to commit to a project or some task that you believe is beyond your ability. It may be something you've been afraid to try but know that God is calling you to do. It may be something that you always wanted to do but "never got around to doing" for various reasons. Commit the project to Jesus and leave the results to him, not focusing at all on the "finish line" but on every step along the way.

If I had succumbed to this fear of failure or success, neither one of my books would have been written, nor would you be reading this right now. What I discovered was that once you let go of your fear and get your ego out of the way of any project, there is room for the inspiration of the Holy Spirit to lead you, and then it becomes an experience much greater than you could have ever dreamed possible.

Keep in mind that "whatever you do, do from the heart, as for the Lord and not for others" (Colossians 3:23). Throughout the process, praise him for his help, praise him for the gifts that he has given you, and praise him even for the mistakes and problems you encounter along the way. It is virtually impossible to have both praise and fear in your heart at the same time.

Fear of being alone. Most psychologists agree that fear of abandonment is a universal fear that we all face. As we experience or perceive any form of rejection throughout our lives, this fear can intensify, leading us to cling to people or make idols out of just about anything to avoid the prospect of being alone or lonely. Sometimes this fear can manifest itself in excessive risk-taking behavior to combat "boredom," which is really a cover-up for deep, abiding restlessness or loneliness. This fear can also lead to addictions, distorted and damaging relationships, and a crippling dependence on things that are not of God. Scripture addresses this condition in the first of the Ten Commandments, which says, "I am the LORD your God. . . . You shall not have other gods beside me" (Exodus 20:2, 3), and again when Jesus says, "No one can serve two masters" (Matthew 6:24).

When we feel crippled with a need for someone or something other than God for our contentment or sense of security, we need to turn to him and his word to make things right. In truth he makes many promises to us and will not abandon us in our neediness. Here are just a few of the reassurances we are given to overcome the fear of being alone and its consequences:

To whom I have said, You are my servant;
I chose you, I have not rejected you—

Do not fear: I am with you;
  do not be anxious: I am your God.
I will strengthen you, I will help you,
  I will uphold you with my victorious right hand.
  (Isaiah 41:9-10)

Blessed is the man who perseveres in temptation, for when
he has been proved he will receive the crown of life that he
promised to those who love him. (James 1:12)

Even if my father and mother forsake me,
  the LORD will take me in. (Psalm 27:10)

Do not fear, for I have redeemed you;
  I have called you by name: you are mine.
When you pass through waters, I will be with you;
  through rivers, you shall not be swept away.
When you walk through fire, you shall not be burned,
  nor will flames consume you. (Isaiah 43:1-2)

Getting to the root of our fear is an important step in our
healing. Here are some common roots of fear:

Childhood trauma, including abuse, neglect, inadequate
bonding, disruption of early attachments, or any other "cat-
astrophic event"—even when we are not consciously aware
of it—can change and affect us physically and emotionally
for the rest of our lives. Many times this manifests itself in
fear, free-floating anxiety, and other phobias or paranoia that

can cause emotional, spiritual, or chemical imbalances. These imbalances may or may not contribute to diagnosable psychiatric or physical conditions but will most definitely affect the interior spiritual state of freedom from fear.

Even normal childhood experiences can create conditions that evoke unresolved fear. If we were not comforted and cared for and our fears went unchecked, they can go "underground," leaving an "open door" in a spiritual sense for Satan to "steal and slaughter and destroy" (John 10:10). A spirit of fear can cripple us in many ways, sometimes without us even being aware of its stronghold on us until it's almost too late. Judy's story illustrates this situation:

I had been so afraid for so long that I thought it was normal. I lived with anxiety all of the time, and it was mostly centered on what I considered my shyness. I was terrified to be noticed, and I constantly worried about what other people thought of me. It never occurred to me that it might be a "spiritual captivity" thing until I found myself going through my second divorce because of my intense insecurity and feelings of jealousy. I was so depressed that I was thinking about taking my own life.

I started seeing a priest, and he began to ask me to talk about rejection in my childhood. At first, I just laughed it off, but he pressed me and I began to make the connection.

When I was four, my parents divorced and my brother went to live with my father. I stayed with my mother, so she was the only family I had. She was depressed and angry most of the time. Somehow I absorbed all of her negativity and came to the conclusion that her unhappiness was my fault. I felt scared and overwhelmed by the weight of her sadness. The priest helped me to realize that I was carrying a burden of fear that was not my own and something that Jesus never intended for me.

When I came to the conclusion that my fear and shyness were not my crosses to bear, I began to pray for release, and I am happy to say that Jesus has answered that prayer!

If you can relate to Judy's story, please know that healing of childhood trauma is possible, and it is crucial to seek this type of healing. Engaging the help of a good therapist, spiritual director, or priest who is gifted in healing is both important and necessary. Asking the Holy Spirit to guide you and praying the prayer at the end of this chapter will help as well. As you get to the root of your fears, you will find comfort in the sacraments, especially as you keep in mind that *every* Mass is a healing Mass.

St. Francis de Sales said that "fear is a greater evil than evil itself."[33] That is a pretty strong statement, indicating that it is worth taking the time and putting the effort into recovery. Fear, more than anything else, robs us of a lifetime of the freedom that Jesus died to give us. So give yourself plenty of time to heal. Such wounds naturally take a long time to heal, so be patient as you go through this healing process.

Unresolved guilt and unrepented sin can lead to excessive fear in our lives. In such cases, fear is the "cover-up" emotion and is often expressed by chronic worry and a spirit of control over people or events. Worriers are controllers, for the most part, because they need to discharge their tension in a way that relieves the negative feelings that drive them. Those negative feelings are misinterpreted as fear instead of guilt. This guilt may be warranted or not, but it has gone underground and unacknowledged, fanning the flames of fear in their lives.

Unacknowledged and unconfessed sin will produce real guilt in the baptized Christian because the Holy Spirit will alert us (via our consciences) if we have gone astray. How we handle, or rather how we mishandle, this "alert" can lead to a proliferation of fear in our lives. Sin separates us from God—it is the only thing that can. Our own free will can lead us into sin and bring us into this state of separation, which is both unnatural and harmful to our souls. Even when we don't believe something is sinful and we participate in the activity that God says is a sin, we will experience the consequence of that sin, which is often a nagging fear that won't go away or let us rest. Keith experienced this kind of fear in his life:

When I was twenty-one, my girlfriend at the time became pregnant. We were both in college and looking forward to fast-track careers in corporate America. A baby was not in the plans, and we both agreed that an abortion was the best option. Though we were both raised Catholic, neither one of us believed that abortion was wrong, and we certainly weren't practicing our religion, so it seemed a simple decision at the time. She had the abortion and everything seemed fine for a while. We graduated from college and went our separate ways.

When I entered the business world, I found the competition uncharacteristically harsh. I had always been in sports and thrived on "being the best," but in the work world, I was really bothered by the cutthroat nature of the relationships with my co-workers. In order to unwind, I found myself drinking nearly every night. I began having nightmares and grew increasingly aggressive with others, especially with my friends and family. I was starting to really unravel and began having panic attacks, but I shared this with no one. For many years I felt as if I was in my own private hell. I attributed it all to stress at work.

I remained in this state for over ten years, until I returned to the Church to marry my wife. During our pre-Cana training, I discovered that it was the sin of the abortion that was driving me down the road of despair I was on. Through the priest, I entered a program for men affected by abortion and I went to confession. Slowly the stress lifted, and I began to make the clear connection. The fear and stress I was feeling was a direct result of the abortion. As painful as it has been to face what I did, I am very grateful to be getting free.

A lack of forgiveness can also contribute to our fears. A harsh and critical attitude has a way of "turning in on itself" and can cripple our own spirits. Jesus warned us of this type of judgment:

"Be merciful, just as [also] your Father is merciful. Stop judging and you will not be judged. Stop condemning and you will not be condemned. Forgive and you will be forgiven. Give and gifts will be given to you; a good measure, packed together, shaken down, and overflowing, will be poured into your lap. For the measure with which you measure will in return be measured out to you." (Luke 6:36-38)

In fact, fear fuels a lack of forgiveness, and unforgiveness keeps us enslaved to those fears. When we are afraid to "lose face" or "give in" or we fear that someone will not apologize or understand our pain, we tend to withhold forgiveness. Sometimes we are afraid to forgive because we think it will give the other person permission to hurt us again, or we mistakenly think that by withholding our forgiveness, we are teaching the other person a lesson. We may feel that it is better to not forgive than to feel vulnerable or appear weak.

At some point in our lives, however, we will need to make the decision and carry it through to *return good in the face of evil*. We must choose our good over someone else's evil, our right over someone else's wrong. We must refuse to let our fears keep us from becoming a forgiving person. And when we do that, it will be like slapping fear in the face! Gary Chapman, in his book *Love Is a Way of Life*, writes: "Fear is a competitor to forgiveness, but it is not as strong as love. When we love others who wrong us, we will find a freedom from our fears that allows us to enjoy our relationships like never before."[34]

Jesus is the only source of restoration for us and the only one who can save us from our fears. We can experience both his healing and his saving grace through the sacraments in a real, complete, and tangible way. Our encounters with Jesus during the Sacrament of Reconciliation and at Mass are a strong defense against fear. We may have to go more than once or go many times, but we can trust that fear will diminish as we participate with our whole hearts in these sacraments of spiritual healing.

For Your Reflection

1. Write down all of your fears, the little ones and the big ones, holding nothing back. Then recite the rosary, and with every bead, release a fear and hand it over to the Blessed Mother so that she can take it to her Son.

2. Read and reflect upon Psalm 6. This psalm is for anyone who struggles with fear.

3. Recite and personalize the following "Prayer for Inner Healing":

Dear Lord Jesus, please come and heal my wounded and troubled heart. I beg you to heal the torments that are causing anxiety in my life. I beg you, in a particular way, to heal the underlying source of my sinfulness. I beg you to come into my life and heal the psychological harms that struck me in my childhood and from the injuries they have caused throughout my life.

Lord Jesus, you know my burdens. I lay them on your Good Shepherd's Heart. I beseech you—by the merits of the great open wound in your Heart—to heal the small wounds that are in mine. Heal my memories, so that nothing that has happened to me will cause me to remain in pain and anguish, filled with anxiety.

Heal, O Lord, all those wounds that have been the cause of evil that is rooted in my life. I want to forgive all those who have offended me. Look to those inner sores that make me unable to forgive. You who came to forgive the afflicted of heart, please, heal my wounded and troubled heart.

Heal, O Lord Jesus, all those intimate wounds that are the root cause of my physical illness. I offer you my heart. Accept it, Lord, purify it, and give me the sentiments of your Divine Heart.

Heal me, O Lord, from the pain caused by the death of my loved ones. Grant me to regain peace and joy in the knowledge that you are the Resurrection and the Life. Make me an authentic witness to your resurrection, your victory over sin and death, and your loving presence among all men. Amen.[35]

Chapter Ten

The Gift of Grief

There is an appointed time for everything. . . .
A time to weep, and a time to laugh;
a time to mourn, and a time to dance.
(Ecclesiastes 3:1, 4)

There's a hole in my heart that is never going to heal—but we are building a fence around it so we don't fall in." That was how one mother described her grief after the murder of her daughter. She and her husband graciously allowed me to interview them for this book. They are both members of a club that none of us ever want to join. The loss of a child through violence is one of the most devastating and difficult crosses that anyone can bear.

Grief is a powerful experience, and grieving is an all-encompassing, inescapable part of life. It is a necessary stop along the way as we begin to address the hurts and betrayals we experience that need forgiveness. Grieving helps us to express the pain of the many losses we may incur as a result of our broken relationships. If we are fortunate enough, grief and the sadness, pain, and loss that it evokes in our hearts will eventually become integrated into the fabric of our lives, like the dark threads in a tapestry or the shadows in a painting. Slowly and gradually, we come out of that darkness to embrace the gifts that grief can bring into our lives.

Sometimes we grieve in the wilderness of having no one to blame but God for the suffering and misfortune we endure. These are the times of the dark night, when we are surrounded by a suffocating aloneness and a torrent of tortured emotions and thoughts. David captures these emotions in the following psalm:

> How long, LORD? Will you utterly forget me?
>   How long will you hide your face from me?
> How long must I carry sorrow in my soul,
>   grief in my heart day after day?
>   How long will my enemy triumph over me?
> Look upon me, answer me, LORD, my God!
>   (Psalm 13:2-4)

No matter how difficult or painful it may be to face our pain, we cannot fully heal without grieving first. When we think of grief, we immediately think of the loss of a loved one through death, yet there are other kinds of loss that we must honor with our grief. Some of these include major life changes or shifts such as aging, illness, job loss, relocation, or the end of any meaningful relationship. We grieve through life's transitions, as when our children grow up and leave the nest, our pet dies, our church closes, or we lose a job.

We must also find the courage to grieve for what should have been but never was and never will be in our lives. We can only make peace with our past to the extent that we are willing to grieve the not-so-happy endings to our life stories: the marriages that ended in divorce, the childhoods that were stolen away by abuse, the mistakes we made that we can never take back.

There are many things that complicate our ability to freely grieve. Some of them may have to do with our temperament, our culture, or our family of origin. We are often given confusing messages about grief and sorrow when we are young. ("Don't cry." "Don't be a baby." "Stop being so sensitive.") As we grow, these misconceptions can get in the way and block our grieving. Here are some truths about grief that can help us understand the grieving process:

Grief is normal. It seems obvious to say that grief is normal, but when we are in the throes of it, many of us respond to grief as if there were something wrong with us. Grief is the natural, human, internal reaction we have to loss in our lives. Bereavement is the state we enter as we experience that loss, and mourning is the outward expression of our loss through emotions, rituals, and behaviors. All of these are necessary to help us heal.

There is no right way or wrong way to grieve. Ever since Elisabeth Kubler-Ross presented her groundbreaking work on the stages of grief in her classic work *On Death and Dying*, there has been a good deal of attention paid to a "prescription for grieving" that includes following the stages she highlighted: denial, anger, bargaining, depression, acceptance. More recent research, however, indicates that "some people go through stages of grief and some people don't, . . . while many of us experience more than one stage or emotion at a time. The result is that grief is more of a process that is associated with a sense of yearning than with sadness or anger."[36] All of this goes to support the idea that there is no right or wrong way to grieve, and that the only negative aspect of bereavement is one in which we don't allow ourselves to experience our emotional pain. The wisdom behind the saying that "the only way around grief is to go through it" can't be underplayed. Our grief needs to be expressed.

Men and women grieve differently. My husband and I experienced our first miscarriage four years into our marriage. It was a devastating blow for us because we were so eager to have a child. Even though my husband and I had a very close relationship and a good, solid marriage, the trauma of losing a child made us feel like strangers. Thankfully, I had read that, in general, men and women grieve differently, and that it is best not to have any expectations, pass judgment, or hold it against someone who is grieving alongside you, especially when he or she seems to be behaving differently than you would expect. This piece of advice probably saved our marriage, especially when we were experiencing the anger phase of grief. By nature and necessity, we took two separate paths toward healing, and after a time, the paths came closer and converged again once we allowed our grief to run its course.

Grief can be very isolating because no two people grieve in exactly the same way—no one can truly understand our pain. Even in a close marriage, there are times when we won't have the energy or desire to care about our spouse's pain because we are so overwhelmed with our own. It doesn't mean that we're not concerned; we just may not be able to be there for one another in the way that we normally would because of the magnitude of our pain. And we may be puzzled by the way our spouse expresses his or her pain. An article written by Mandy Tanner from the Natural Parenting Group entitled "Understanding Gender Differences and Grief" gives a helpful comparison:

Understanding His Grief:
- Do not expect tears, but understand that there is an intensity of emotion.
- Do not expect him to use words to describe his feelings.
- Expect a need to intellectualize and problem solve as a means of making sense of the loss and the new world faced.
- Accept and respect the need for privacy and solitude. This is not a rejection of your support but rather the need for a sense of independence and control over the loss.
- Accept and respect the focus and investment of energy on the future rather than the past. This is a way of integrating the loss into life.

Understanding Her Grief:
- Expect lots of tears; they are natural and normal, and you do not need to stop them.
- Respect the need to share and communicate about the loss as a source of comfort. This is not a search for answers but a means to make sense of the new world faced.
- Accept and respect the need for social support. This is not a betrayal of intimate relationships or a rejection

of support already offered; it is an ongoing need for social connections.

- Accept and respect the focus and investment in the past; this is a way to hold onto connections of the loss.[37]

Grief is a uniquely felt and often solitary experience. One powerful account of what grief feels like comes from C. S Lewis in his book *A Grief Observed*:

No one ever told me that grief felt so like fear. I am not afraid, but the sensation is like being afraid. The same fluttering in the stomach, the same restlessness, the yawning. I keep on swallowing. At other times it feels like being mildly drunk, or concussed. There is a sort of invisible blanket between the world and me. I find it hard to take in what anyone says. . . . And grief still feels like fear. Perhaps more strictly, like suspense. Or like waiting; just hanging about waiting for something to happen. It gives life a permanently provisional feeling. It doesn't seem worth starting anything. I can't settle down. I yawn, I fidget, I smoke too much. Up till this I always had too little time. Now there is nothing but time. Almost pure time, empty successiveness. . . .[38]

Grief can't be rushed. We can be grieving long after our mourning is over. There is no magic number of months or years that mark the end of our grieving, so don't feel ashamed if even well-meaning people tell you to "get over it," and you can't. One of the best books I have ever read on grief is *Tear*

Soup by Pat Schweibert and Chuck DeKlyen, in which they point out that "most people can tolerate another's loss for about a month before wanting the bereaved person to get back to normal."[39] Certainly that is unrealistic because grief takes lots of emotional energy and time.

Nevertheless, there is something that grief experts call "complicated" or "traumatic" grief. This is grief that is characterized by a deep and intractable mourning. With complicated grief, there is no gradual diminishing of the emotional impact of the loss or resolution but a sustained sense of disbelief or denial, yearning, and emotional pain. A person who is struggling with complicated grief will either put off grieving altogether or experience all of the symptoms of grieving but to the extreme and for a prolonged period of time. The person may even experience the same symptoms as post-traumatic stress disorder, including extreme agitation, intense sensitivity to stimulus, and uncontrolled and unwanted thoughts.[40]

Complicated grief is not always the result of a person's lack of ability to cope but is more often related to the nature of the relationship that the bereaved had with the person who died. Extenuating circumstances such as a violent death, suicide, or unresolved issues in the relationship are more likely to contribute to complicated grief. The best way to help someone who is struggling with complicated grief is to listen and encourage him or her to seek out a professional therapist. People cannot usually resolve this type of grief on their own.

When my friend committed suicide, I found myself in need of support, and so I attended a bereavement group especially for survivors of suicide. In that group I noticed one woman who seemed to be struggling more than the rest of us (or at least showing it more). She was softly weeping throughout the whole group session. When it came time for her to share, I was surprised to find out that she had lost her loved one three years earlier but had not dealt with the pain until shortly before she attended the group. "I thought I was doing fine, but I wasn't," she said. "It hit me all of a sudden with a force that knocked me over." The cascade of her tears was like a dammed-up waterfall that could no longer be contained.

It's very important to get help with unexpressed grief because it has the potential to make us sick. As one study states, "Subjects with traumatic grief are at increased risk of developing cancers and other illnesses. Should grief remain unresolved, this vulnerability becomes part of the individual's nervous system."[41] The reality of the importance of grieving, therefore, affects not only our minds and hearts but our bodies as well.

A wise writer once wrote, "We would rather explain our hurt than feel it."[42] When we grieve at the deepest level, we are giving up all our defenses, all our fantasies, and even our hidden hopes for things to be different, until there is nothing left but raw pain. It's no wonder that we try to avoid it, but we will all have the opportunity to master the art of grieving in our lifetimes. Holocaust survivor Etty Hillesum suggests just how important this grief work can be: "Give your sorrow all the space and shelter in yourself that is its due, for if everyone bears his grief honestly and courageously, the sorrow that now fills the world will abate."[43]

In many ways, when we grieve, we "die to self" in a spiritual sense. We do this over and over again as we come face-to-face with our inner pain and suffering. The whole of our faith is based on the truth that Jesus destroyed our death when he died and restored our life when he rose from the dead. When we face our losses and grieve fully, we can hope in the rising again, in the resurrection and restoration that Jesus died to give us. Whether you have survived a painful childhood, endured a broken relationship, suffered a devastating loss, or have been deeply wounded in some other way, when you finally embrace the sorrow, you will find peace in the midst of your storm.

In the Sermon on the Mount, Jesus said it plainly: "Blessed are they who mourn, / for they will be comforted" (Matthew 5:4). Grieving people often report "supernatural" gifts of comfort, which some attribute to the Holy Spirit or to angels, God's holy messengers. Carol, who lost her son, experienced this:

Our son died on a Friday around 3:00 in the afternoon after suffering terribly for several days. As we were driving home from the hospital that night, I was suddenly flooded with the thought that Mary's son was murdered too. I know that I was given that thought to carry me through. I felt protected and supported and not alone.

So did my friend Adele, who lost her husband, Bernardo, to lung cancer just before her youngest daughter's eighteenth birthday. He was trying very hard to hang on so that he could join them on the special trip they had planned for the occasion at a nearby resort. It wasn't meant to be. Devastated and in the throes of early raging grief, my friend was anguished at the thought of having to carry through with the plans without her husband. Yet she did not want to let her daughter down, and she knew how important it was to continue living even though she was dying inside. The day came, and the two of them entered the resort. Almost immediately, Adele was drawn to the melody playing over the loudspeaker in the lobby. It was an obscure Bee Gees song, "To Love Somebody." But it wasn't just any song, it was "their song," and even in the depth of her pain, Adele was comforted, sensing that Bernardo was truly with them.

Let it be a comfort for you to know that we are never alone in our grief, even when it feels that way. Jesus himself experienced grief at the tomb of his friend Lazarus. We serve a God who shed tears over the death of his friend and over the state and condition of Jerusalem. Jesus "offered prayers and supplications with loud cries and tears" to God (Hebrews 5:7). He experienced the same yearning for comfort and relief in the garden of Gethsemane that we long for when we feel that we are going to die from the depths of our sorrow. The Gospel of Mark describes the scene: "He . . . began to be troubled and distressed. Then he said to them, 'My soul is sorrowful even to death'" (14:33-34). It's no wonder that Jesus is described as "a man of suffering" in the Book of Isaiah (53:3).

Blessed are those who mourn, for they will be comforted. We don't need to fear our grief. God will give us the strength to face our Gethsemane moments. Even at their deepest, darkest depths, our sorrows can lead to joy, our deaths, to new life. These are truly the gifts of grief: that we will be drawn closer to the heart of Jesus and that we will be comforted in our sorrow. Let him heal you in your grief and restore you to a wholeness that you have yet to imagine.

1. Draw a timeline of your life from your birth to the present, and highlight your major losses. This could include people who have died, as well as other major losses in your life. Reflect on how you grieved and honored those losses in your life. Did you take the time to grieve? How have these losses affected your life? How have they become a part of your life? Keeping with the image of your life as a tapestry and the dark threads as your losses, what beauty and light have come into your life to contrast the "dark threads" of sorrow and loss? *What gifts have you been given along your road to healing?*

2. When we are hurting, we need our mother, and each one of us has the comfort and care of our Blessed Mother available to us. There are many beautiful depictions of Mary as our sorrowful mother and prayers to accompany this devotion. What I found particularly helpful and comforting as I was grieving the loss of my three children to miscarriage was a meditation on the Seven Sorrows of Our Lady:

   1. The Prophecy of Simeon. (Luke 2:34-35)
   2. The Flight into Egypt. (Matthew 2:13-15)
   3. The Loss of the Child Jesus in the Temple. (Luke 2:43-46)

4. Mary Meets Jesus on the Way to Calvary. (Luke 23:27)
5. Jesus Dies on the Cross. (John 19:25-30)
6. Mary Receives the Body of Jesus in Her Arms. (Matthew 27:57-59)
7. The Body of Jesus Is Placed in the Tomb. (John 19:40-42)

Say one Hail Mary while reflecting on each of the seven sorrows every day. It is a simple devotion but has great graces for healing available for those who embrace it.

3. Read the following psalms, all of which have something to do with mourning and grief: Psalms 23, 27, 30, 42, 116. Then write your own psalm of mourning.

Chapter Eleven

Some Final Thoughts

There is a short sentence buried in Scripture with a profound message. Jesus spoke it in the presence of a house full of very important people and one lowly woman, who washed his feet with her tears. He said, "The one to whom little is forgiven, loves little" (Luke 7:47).

Perhaps that is the essence of this whole book. Our healing is really about making our love "bigger." It is about enlarging our hearts to embrace life's tragedies with the triumphs, to make peace with the pain that we have endured and that we have caused others, and to be reconciled by the flow of God's grace and mercy, moment by moment. We are moving through our lives toward an end point that we call death. Yet in our spirits we are hopeful, and by faith we believe that this death will lead to a new life and our ultimate and complete healing. This is the promise of our salvation and the purpose of our lives.

My friends, it is worth the journey! Even as your hurts cry out for healing, so does God's reply of mercy, hope, and transforming love. If there is anything I hope to have communicated through this book, it is that you are loved and that you are not alone, no matter how much you are hurting. God's healing flows from heaven in a shower of graces meant just for you.

Probably the most profound bit of insight I received through the writing of this book came from Lucy, the mother whose daughter was murdered. She said it quite clearly that the cross of grief that she is carrying is like the one that Jesus talks about when he says, "My yoke is easy, and my burden light" (Matthew 11:30):

It is Satan who wants to give us the heavier cross. He wants us to carry the hatred and bitterness around until it destroys us, and he never helps. But Jesus is always there right alongside us, helping us with our crosses, making them lighter with his love. I could never bear my pain without him.

Hers is a wisdom born of sorrow, but it is a truth that sets her free.

Peace is possible, and it is nearer than you think. It comes in the form of a Person: Jesus Christ, whose presence can penetrate the closed doors of your heart and break down the walls of your pain and fear. He did it for the disciples in their confusion and sorrow after his crucifixion, and he can do it today for you.

Our Lord is intimately interested in restoring you to wholeness and joy and reconciling your broken relationships. Will you open your heart to receive him? I pray that you will work with his grace and allow him to heal you and speak to you those beautiful words that he spoke to the sorrowful woman in Luke's Gospel: "Your faith has saved you; go in peace" (Luke 7:50).

PART THREE

HEALING PRAYERS AND RESOURCES

Prayer is like having a meeting with God. When we invest our time and engage our hearts in the conversation, there is power in our prayers, and they can change things for us in a mighty way. Commit yourself to a life of prayer, and your hurts will lose their sting. Start and end each day with prayer, and when you think of it, pray during the day. Use these prayers here as "conversation starters" with God, and allow the Holy Spirit to guide you and inspire you as you pour out your heart to him.

This part of the book also includes a sampling of resources (mostly Catholic) that may be of help to you on your journey. While I am familiar with most of these resources and have gathered them through trusted Web sites, their inclusion here does not constitute an endorsement by me or by the publisher of this book. Be sure to go to your priest or a trusted spiritual adviser or friend if you need more information on these organizations.

HEALING PRAYERS

PRAYER FOR ENLIGHTENMENT FROM THE HOLY SPIRIT

Dear Holy Spirit, my Advocate, Counselor, and Friend, I call on you now to open my mind and heart to your wisdom and guidance as I seek *freedom, forgiveness,* and *healing* in my life. Help me to be honest and authentic in my self-reflections and courageous in the face of any fears, obstacles, or trials. Give me a heart full of hope to receive your healing light and the peace that comes from knowing you and following your ways all the days of my life. Amen.

PRAYER OF HEALING FOR CHRONIC ANGER

Dear Lord, I need your help to openly, honestly, and effectively handle my anger. I know that my emotions are a gift from you, and I want to receive them in a way that is life-giving and that brings honor to you. Don't let my anger be a stumbling block or a source of sin, but purify it in the burning fires of your love. I especially need help with my anger toward_____. Lord, I long to do your will, and I know that you do not want me to be an angry or bitter person. Release me from any strongholds of a spirit of anger, and replace them with bonds of compassion, humility, and love. Amen.

Prayer for Release from a Spirit of Fear

Dear Lord, I am afraid of so many things, and my spirit is restless with anxiety! This fear is such a burden, and I long for your peace. Guide me to a place of inner calm, and grant me serenity and a quiet mind. Lord, you are greater than all of my fears put together, and I trust in you.

Mary, my Mother, protect me from all anxiety and the insecurities that cripple my spirit. Plead with your Son for my release from the bondage of fear. I believe that the perfect love of Jesus casts out fear, and I claim it. He has promised me an abundant life and a peace that surpasses all understanding.

Lord, I am handing over all of my fears to you, especially _____. Fill me with the grace to let them go and walk in the light of your freedom and perfect love. Amen.

Prayer for a Grieving Heart

Dear Lord, my heart is breaking for the loss that I feel in my life right now. It seems that nothing will ever feel normal or good for me again. I am lonely, scared, and filled with sorrow. No matter where I turn, I cannot find comfort or rest. All seems dark and hopeless. Still, I know that you are with me and that you, too, have felt alone and abandoned. Please send your consolation. Help me to feel your presence like a loving embrace. Help me to see and encounter you in the loving and caring gestures of others. Lord, rescue me from this pit of grief, and moment by moment, day by day, build me back up with your unending love. Amen.

Prayer for Physical Healing

Heavenly Father, my body is your creation, and you have filled it with strength, wisdom, and a mysterious perfection that is far beyond the capacity of my mind to understand. Even now as I am suffering this physical ailment, I believe in the power of your healing and your loving heart that wants to restore me to wholeness. So I ask you now for a healing of mind, body, and spirit that will bring glory to your name. I know that I am in your care and that you will never leave me. Thank you, Father, for blessing me with the gift of your healing love. Amen

Prayer for Spiritual Healing and Wholeness

Lord, I have been struggling; my spirit is dark and heavy, and I feel broken inside. There is so much that I do not understand, and it overwhelms me. Still, it brings me comfort to know that you are in control of the process of healing and self-discovery that will lead me to spiritual freedom. Your timing and ways are perfect and your knowledge is complete. Heal me in my spirit, in the innermost part of by being. Release me from the past and heal my memories. Tend to the roots of my soul sickness so that I can give and receive love freely and rest in the secure arms of your embrace. Restore me, Lord, that I may live as you would have me live—with a heart full of joy and a spirit full of love. Amen.

Prayer of Recovery from a Deep Wound

Oh my Jesus, the pain that I have endured is immense. Sometimes I think I cannot bear it. It seems this wound is too deep for words and that it will never go away. How can I live with it? How can I go on? And even as I speak these words, I am reminded of your own wounds that you showed to the apostles in the Upper Room after the resurrection. It gives me hope to know that I, too, can rise from the depth of this despair. Lord, show me the way. Lift me up and lance this wound with your love. I promise to persevere in my recovery and lean on you for strength along the way. Lord, you are my wounded healer; set me free. Amen.

Prayer of Reconciliation

Lord, your ways are above my own, and my understanding often fails me. Where I see broken relationships, you see the potential for something brand-new. When I am hopelessly locked in anger or discouragement, your heart holds the key to restoration. You long for unity even when I work toward a selfish end or refuse to forgive. Lord, teach me your ways and help me to be more like you. Let mercy reign in my heart, and help me to always be open to your reconciling love. Show me when I am being stubborn. Fill me with your wisdom. Give me the courage to confess my sins. Infuse a spirit of humility in me so that reconciliation will be possible in every area of my life, in accordance with your will. Amen.

Prayer for the Grace to Forgive

Precious Jesus, you know my heart and you know how hard it is sometimes for me to forgive, especially in the situation with _____. Help me to forgive in a way that brings dignity to us both and honor to you. Send your Holy Spirit to remind me of the ways in which I need forgiveness, and prepare my heart to receive your mercy in my brokenness. Lord, I know that freedom comes through forgiveness and I want that freedom, so please fill me with an overflow of your grace and show me how to forgive. Amen.

Prayer for the Grace to Forgive Oneself

Lord, have mercy on me, a sinner. Do not let me hold onto my sin more tightly than I grab hold of your amazing grace. You died so that I could walk in freedom from shame and the bondage of sin. You died so that I could live. Lord, when I am despairing and punishing myself with guilt and condemnation, I am ignoring your gift of mercy. I vow to receive your grace to forgive myself and move on down the road to healing. Thank you, Lord, for your forgiveness and your merciful heart. Amen.

Prayer of Praise and Thanksgiving

Thank you, Jesus. My heart is overflowing with gratitude. I am thankful for your unchanging care and concern for my every need. I praise you for your perfect ways and your perfect love. Lord, I am filled with joy for the gift of my life, and I vow to live it in obedience to your word and in celebration of your love. Holy Spirit, you are the friend closest to my heart, and I am grateful for your wise counsel and companionship. God, my Father and Creator, I am blessed beyond measure, and I worship and adore you with all of my heart. Amen.

Healing Resources

National Life Center Crisis Pregnancy Center Hotline: 1–800–848–LOVE.

Project Rachel. Offering hope and healing for those grieving abortion: www.hopeafterabortion.com.

Silent No More. The Silent No More Awareness Campaign is an effort to make the public aware of the devastation abortion brings to women, men, and their families: www.silent -nomoreawareness.org.

Abuse

National Domestic Violence Hotline: 1–800–799–SAFE.

National Child Abuse Hotline: 1–800–4–A–CHILD.

Abused Women. A Comprehensive Web site containing information and helpful resources for any woman who is trying to get out of an abusive relationship: www.abusedwomen .org/resources.html.

Calix Society. An association of Catholic alcoholics who are maintaining their sobriety through affiliation with and participation in the Fellowship of Alcoholics Anonymous: www.calixsociety.org/

Sober Catholic Blog. An interactive blog/discussion site that focuses on alcoholism and sobriety/recovery from a Catholic perspective: www.sobercatholic.com.

Sober for Christ. A Catholic lay apostolate that reaches out to Catholic Christians who are afflicted with addictions: www.soberforchrist.com.

Alcoholics Anonymous: www.aa.org.

Al-Anon & Alateen: www.al-anon.alateen.org.

Adult Children of Alcoholics: www.adultchildren.org.

Cocaine Anonymous: www.ca.org.

Narcotics Anonymous: www.na.org.

Overeaters Anonymous: www.oa.org.

Sexual Addicts Anonymous: www.saa-recovery.org.

Scrupulous Anonymous: mission.liguori.org/newsletters/scrupanon.htm.

Pornography Addiction: www.thekingsmen.us/; www.dads.org/strugglewithporn.asp; www.whodoesithurt.com/home.

BEREAVEMENT

National Catholic Ministry to the Bereaved: 1–314–638–2639; www.griefwork.org.

Grief Watch. A Web site created to provide bereavement resources, memorial products, and links that can help through a personal loss: www.griefwatch.com.

Creighton University Web Site of Grief Resources: onlineministries.creighton.edu/CollaborativeMinistry/Grief.

MISCARRIAGE AND CHILD LOSS

Share Pregnancy and Infant Loss Support. An organization that serves those whose lives are touched by the death of a baby through early pregnancy loss, stillbirth, or in the first few months of life: www.nationalshare.org.

The Apostolate of Hannah's Tears. A blog dedicated to support and prayer for the sanctity of marriage and family

through the trials of infertility and miscarriage: hannahstears
.net

National Suicide Hope Line: 1–800–784–2433.

American Foundation for Suicide Prevention. An organization dedicated to reducing loss of life from suicide through research and education: www.afsp.org.

For Suicide Survivors. A Web site designed by survivors for survivors of suicide devoted to those who are grieving the loss of a loved one by suicide: www.allianceofhope.org.

Spiritual Survivors. A spiritual support group located in the Denver area for adult survivors of sexual assault as well as an ecumenical online resource: www.spiritualsurvivors.com.

COUNSELING, COACHING, EMOTIONAL HEALING

Catholic Therapists. An online resource and directory of Catholic therapists who are loyal to the magisterial teachings of the Catholic Church: www.catholictherapists.com.

Catholic Spiritual Direction. Provides a ministry of personal spiritual direction in the Roman Catholic tradition through the Internet, by email, and by telephone in order to provide this ministry to those who are unable (by reason of job, family situation, or location) to have the benefit of direction face-to-face: www.catholicspiritualdirection.org.

Catholic Spiritual/Motivational Coaching. My own Web site and blog highlighting offerings of healing/inspirational presentations, workshops, and missions: www.charismatacoaching.com.

Affirmation Therapy. A Web site dedicated to the work of the late Catholic psychiatrist, author, and lecturer Dr. Conrad W. Baars: www.conradbaars.com/affirmation-therapy.htm.

Depression

Beyond Blue. An online daily weblog by Theresa Borchard, Catholic author and presenter, who shares her own spiritual journey to mental health as a person diagnosed with bipolar disorder. This weblog provides resources and encouragement for all types of mental illness and recovery strategies: blog .beliefnet.com/beyondblue.

Spiritual Warfare and Healing

Healing Power Ministries. The personal healing ministry of Robert Abel, who was miraculously healed after a devastating accident involving a drunk driver. www.healingpower-ministries.com/default.htm and www. catholicwarriors. com.

Heart of the Father Ministries. Run by Neal Lozano and his wife, Janet, this organization offers "UnBound: Freedom in Christ" conferences and materials on deliverance prayer: heartofthefather.com.

Archangel St. Raphael Holy Healing Ministry. Healing ministry and apostolate promoting Jesus' healing message of love, reconciliation and forgiveness, founded by Fr. Joseph Whalen: www.straphaeloil.com.

Christian Healing Ministries. A healing ministry founded by Francis MacNutt, author of several best-selling books on healing prayer, and his wife, Judith: www.christianhealingmin.org.

MARRIAGE AND FAMILY

Pastoral Solutions Institute. An organization founded by Greg Popcak providing resources and telephone counseling to Catholics on marriage and family life: www.exceptional-marriages.com.

St. Joseph's Covenant Keepers. An informal international network of Christian men, under the patronage of St. Joseph, dedicated to strengthening the family: www.dads.org.

Women of Grace. An outreach founded by Johnette S. Benkovic to encourage and affirm women in their dignity as daughters of God and in their gift of authentic femininity: www.womenofgrace.com.

Couple to Couple League. An international Catholic non-profit organization dedicated to promoting and teaching fertility awareness (natural family planning) to married and engaged couples: www.ccli.org.

Apostolate for Family Consecration. An international Catholic lay movement founded by Jerry and Gwen Coniker in 1975, created to consecrate families to the Holy Family and in the truths of the Catholic faith: www.familyland.org.

Family Life Center International. Provides resources geared toward deepening a family's love and knowledge of their faith, with a special focus on fatherhood: www.familylifecenter.net.

Retrouvaille. For couples with marital problems, including those who are considering marriage separation or who are already separated or divorced and who want marriage help: www.retrouvaille.org.

ADDITIONAL CATHOLIC SITES

Friends of St. John the Caregiver. An international Catholic organization addressing the growing needs of family caregivers: www.fsjc.org; www.youragingparent.com; www.catholic-caregivers.com.

Guild of St. Benedict Joseph Labre. An apostolate of spiritual support for the emotionally troubled, those with depression and mental illnesses, and their family and friends: guildbjla-bre.com/

Apostolate for People with Chronic Illness or with Disabilities. A way for people with chronic illness or disability to care for others like themselves through an online or postal service Christian support group. Administered by Fr. Lawrence Jagdfeld, OFM: http://www.cusan.org.

Divine Mercy. Four unique lay apostolates of the Marians of the Immaculate Conception that work together with the National Shrine of The Divine Mercy and the Association of Marian Helpers in Stockbridge, Massachusetts. They promote and teach the authentic forms of the message and devotion to The Divine Mercy: thedivinemercy.org.

Endnotes

1. Stormie O'Martian, *Finding Peace for Your Heart* (Nashville: Thomas Nelson Publishers, 1991), 196.

2. Etty Hillesum, K.A.D. Smelik, and Arnold Pomerans, *Etty: The Letters and Diaries of Etty Hillesum 1941–1943* (Grand Rapids: William B. Eerdmans Publishing Company, 2002), 308.

3. M.H. Teicher, "Wounds That Time Won't Heal: The Neurobiology of Child Abuse." *Cerebrum: The Dana Forum on Brain Science*, 2(4), 50–67.

4. Marcel Proust, www.great-quotes.com.

5. "Teaching Clinical Psychology," John Suler, PhD, Ryder University, accessed September 22, 2010, www-usr.rider.edu/~suler/defenses.

6. Desmond Tutu, *No Future without Forgiveness* (New York: Doubleday, 1999), 271.

7. Mark R. McMinn, *Psychology, Theology, and Spirituality in Christian Counseling* (Carol Stream, Illinois: Tyndale House Publishers, 1996), 213.

8. Tom Valeo, "Forgive and Forget," WebMD (2007): 1, www.webmd.com/balance/guide/forgive-forget.

9. "Forgiveness and Health," http://www.forgivenessandhealth.com/html/benefits.html.

10. "Forgiveness and Health."

11. Martin Luther King, www.great-quotes.com.

12. "Unforgiveness is the cause . . . ," www.presentationministries.com/brochures/UnforgivenessCause.asp.

13. Lewis B. Smedes, *The Art of Forgiving: When You Need to Forgive and Don't Know How* (New York: Ballantyne Books, 1996), 137.

14. Henry Cloud and John Townsend, *Boundaries* (Grand Rapids: Zondervan Publishing House, 1992), 134.

15. Julie Exline, PhD, and Simon Rego, PsyD, "Anger toward God: Social-Cognitive Predictors, Prevalence, and Links with Adjustment to Bereavement and Cancer," *Journal of Personality and Social Psychology,* January 2011.

16. Paul Froese and Christopher Bader, "America's Four Gods," www.thearda.com/whoisyourgod/fourgods/distant.asp.

17. Anne Costa, *Refresh Me, Lord! Meditations to Renew a Woman's Spirit* (Frederick, MD: The Word Among Us Press, 2008), 123.

18. "The Nature and Attributes of God," Catholic Encyclopedia, www.newadvent.org/cathen/06612a.htm.

19. Encyclical Letter of Pope John Paul II, *Dives in Misericordia*, 13, issued Nov. 13, 1980, www.vatican.va.

20. Wendy Beckett, *The Gaze of Love: Meditations on Art and Spiritual Transformation* (SanFrancisco: Harper Collins, 1993), 10.

21. St. Maria Faustina Kowalska, *Diary: Divine Mercy in My Soul* (Stockbridge, MA: Marians of the Immaculate Conception, 1987), 282.

22. St. Maria Faustina Kowalska, 292.

23. St. Maria Faustina Kowalska, 297–298.

24. St. Maria Faustina Kowalska, 473.

25. Paul Scanlon, OP, "The Difficulty of Forgiving Ourselves," *Spiritual Life*, vol. 57, no. 1, Spring 2011, 45.

26. Paul Scanlon, OP, 45.

27. Bill Wilson and Dr. Bob Smith, *Alcoholics Anonymous*, 4th ed. (New York: Alcoholics Anonymous World Services, 2001), 59.

28. Henry Cloud and John Townsend, *Boundaries*, 32.

29. Stephanie Holland, "The Anatomy of Anger and Its Effect on Your Health," last modified September 29, 2010,

www.suite101.com/content
/the-anatomy-of-anger-and-its-effect-on-your-health-a291332.

30. www.yourdictionary.com/grudge.

31. www.famousquotesandauthors.com/authors/william_h__
walton_quotes.html.

32. Yoichi Chida and Andrew Steptoe, "The Association of Anger
and Hostility with Future Coronary Artery Disease," *Journal
of the American College of Cardiology*, March 11, 2009, vol.
53:945.

33. Carol Kelly-Gangi, ed., *The Essential Wisdom of the Saints*
(New York: Fall River Press, 2008), 75.

34. Gary Chapman, *Love as a Way of Life (*New York:
Doubleday, 2008), 79.

35. Gabriele Amorth, *An Exorcist Tells His* Story (San Francisco,
California: Ignatius Press, 1999), 201–202.

36. Paul K. Maciejewski, PhD; Baohui Zhang, MS; Susan
D. Block, MD; Holly G. Prigerson, PhD, "An Empirical
Examination of the Stage Theory of Grief," *Journal of the
American Medical Association*, February 21, 2007.

37. Mandy Tanner, "Understanding Gender Differences and
Grief," www.naturalparenting.com.au/flex
/gender-and-grief-how-men-and-women-handle-grief/7818/1.

38. C.S. Lewis, *A Grief Observed* (New York: Bantam Books,
1961), 1, 38–39.

39. Pat Schweibert and Chuck DeKlyen, *Tear Soup* (Portland:
Griefwatch Publishers, 1999), 49.

40. www.4therapy.com/life-topics/grief-loss/sometimes
-grief-becomes-complicated-unresolved-or-stuck-2249.

41. Mary Lou Bernardo, "When Grief Becomes a Disorder," *The
National Psychologist*, May/June, 1998, vol. 1, no. 3.

42. Wayne Muller, *Legacy of the Heart: Spiritual Advantages of a
Painful Childhood* (New York: Simon & Shuster, 1992), 5.

43. Etty Hillesum, *An Interrupted Life and Letters from Westerbork* (New York: Henry Holt, 1996), 97.

the **WORD** among us®
The *Spirit* of Catholic Living

This book was published by The Word Among Us. Since 1981, The Word Among Us has been answering the call of the Second Vatican Council to help Catholic laypeople encounter Christ in the Scriptures.

The name of our company comes from the prologue to the Gospel of John and reflects the vision and purpose of all of our publications: to be an instrument of the Spirit, whose desire is to manifest Jesus' presence in and to the children of God. In this way, we hope to contribute to the Church's ongoing mission of proclaiming the gospel to the world so that all people would know the love and mercy of our Lord and grow ever more deeply in love with him.

Our monthly devotional magazine, *The Word Among Us*, features meditations on the daily and Sunday Mass readings, and currently reaches more than one million Catholics in North America and another half million Catholics in one hundred countries around the world. Our book division, The Word Among Us Press, publishes numerous books, Bible studies, and pamphlets that help Catholics grow in their faith.

To learn more about who we are and what we publish, log on to our website at www.wau.org. There you will find a variety of Catholic resources that will help you grow in your faith.

Embrace His Word, Listen to God . . .

www.wau.org